CERVANTES

CERVANTES

THE LIFE OF A GENIUS

---

by Fernando Diaz-Plaja

translated from the Spanish

by Sue Matz Soterakos

CHARLES SCRIBNER'S SONS / NEW YORK

To Nell and Aurora Díaz-Plaja

"Children are half one's soul; but
daughters are the most complete half."

Cervantes: *La entretenida*

(Act III)

C 3

CONTENTS

PROLOGUE

This is a sad story; the story of a man who gave to the world in general and to his native land, Spain, in particular, a most valuable literary legacy. His creation, *The Ingenious Gentleman, Don Quixote of La Mancha*, has placed him, along with Shakespeare, at the pinnacle of universal writers.

Creative geniuses who have been ignored by their contemporaries are infinite in number. All too frequently their literary or artistic capacities are discovered after their death. But what distinguishes Cervantes' life from that of so many great artists is that his work was anything but ignored during his lifetime. On the contrary, his fame extended beyond national borders almost immediately upon publication of the *Quixote*. His success as a novelist was impressive and he was able to enjoy it while still living.

Nevertheless, because of a series of dramatic circumstances which I shall attempt to describe in the following pages, his artistic and intellectual triumph was not followed by material prosperity. Even after his literary victory he had to contend with a select group of the most famous writers of the day. These men viewed him as being unworthy to associate with them.

During his lifetime Cervantes suffered prison terms and persecutions, physical wounds and spiritual wounds. Each time that he seemed to be getting ahead, the world dealt him some new blow. For this reason I have named his story "The Battered Life of a Genius."

Throughout his literary works are many scenes that correspond to events in his personal life. Wherever it has been possible I have incorporated them into this biography. Who would dare to clothe in other words that which has been written by Don Miguel de Cervantes Saavedra?

INTRODUCTION

The Spain of 1566 was a Spain created by a miracle. Only one century earlier the country did not exist as a political entity. Castile, Aragon, and Navarre fought sporadically over boundaries with the Moors, who were still fortified in their last bastion, the province of Granada, and also along the coast of Málaga. Nobles and bandits, who were sometimes the same, contested the power of the kings.

With the coming to the throne of the "Catholic Kings," Ferdinand and Isabella, dramatic changes rocked the peninsula. The nobles were pressed into the service of the monarchy. A competent federal police force known as the Holy Brotherhood assured safety on the highways. Religious unity was achieved by the expulsion of the Jews just three months after the capture of the last Moorish kingdom in Granada in 1492, and the annexation of Navarre in 1512 resulted in the political unity of the peninsula. It was in this same period that Christopher Columbus, by his discovery of America (known then as the Indies), provided a fantastic outlet for these newly joined forces. In Spain's wars with France she was successful in occupying the southern part of Italy.

As if all of this were not enough, the new king, Charles I of Spain (he was also Charles V of the Holy Roman Empire), who came into power in 1519, inherited from his paternal grandfather the empire which added to Spain's territories the large province of Franche-Conté in north-eastern France, the Low Countries (Belgium, Holland, and Luxembourg), Austria, and the Duchy of Milan. This last assured Spanish containment of the Italian peninsula— Sicily and Naples to the south, Milan in the north, and the rest of it—in what is known today as a sphere of influence.

This incredible expansion in such a short time, this emergence of a country destroyed by interior wars and social problems into a unified power that dominated the then-known world, forged two enduring characteristics of the Spaniard: one, his pride—the arrogance of a people who suddenly found themselves rulers of a world which until then had been unknown to them; the other, a conviction that this unexpected good fortune must be a reward from God for the Catholicism of the Spaniards. Therefore they felt an obligation to carry on as champions of the Catholic faith—first, against the Moslems; second, against the Protestants (Martin Luther had died the year before Cervantes' birth).

The insistence on associating patriotic demands with religion eventually brought about the fall of Spain as a great power. During the entire sixteenth century and a large part of the seventeenth, until her economy could bear no more, Spain felt herself obligated to defend the Catholic religion wherever it might be attacked, even though such a course might be detrimental to her national interests. King Philip II went so far as to say that he would rather not rule at all than rule over a nation of heretics (that is, non-Catholics). For this reason the country became involved in continuous wars. If the Spaniards were not defending themselves against the enemy for patriotic reasons, they were defending their religion in Germany or in Flanders. In spite of the enormous wealth arriving from the New World, and notwithstanding the valor of Spain's soldiers, the time came when she could no longer sustain such tension, and the beginnings of her decline became obvious.

Sometimes Spain's enemy and the enemy of the Catholic faith were the same. For example, the Moslems, whether they were Turks, Algerians, Berber pirates, or Lebanese, were all Mohammedans, that is, members of the Islamic faith, and as such, were adversaries of the religion of Christ. They were also bitter enemies of the Spain which had vanquished the Arabs in 1492.

The same was true of the English under Queen Elizabeth I. They were Anglicans, mortal foes of the Spanish "papists." The English, frustrated in their desire to trade with the Spanish overseas colonies because their king prohibited it, made pirate attacks upon them, as well as upon Spanish galleons returning to the peninsula loaded with gold and silver.

In this atmosphere of incredible Spanish power, menaced by the Turk and by the Protestant, whether English or Dutch, the life of Cervantes unfolded. Symbol of the essence of his country, he was to see the rise of Spanish power (with the battle of Lepanto in 1571, and the annexation of Portugal in 1580), and then its fall (after the defeat of the Invincible Spanish Armada in 1588). Incomparable witness, he was to reflect in the *Quixote* the impact of illusions in conflict with reality: It is a conflict that bears a close resemblance to his own life.

SELF-PORTRAIT
OF CERVANTES

———◆◄►◆———

"He whom you see here with the aquiline countenance, the chestnut hair, the smooth brow, merry eyes, the nose hooked but well proportioned; the silvery beard which less than twenty years ago was golden; large moustache, small mouth, the teeth not much, only six of them and these in poor condition and badly placed with no two of them corresponding to any other two; his figure between two extremes, neither tall nor short, high coloring, more to fair than to dark, somewhat stooped in the shoulders, and not too light on his feet, this I tell you is the author of the *Galatea* and of *Don Quixote of the Mancha*. . . ."

(Prologue, *Exemplary Novels*)

THE YOUNG POET

1566. Madrid, capital of a world which extended from the Italian coast to that of the Pacific, capital of the fabulous Spanish empire, was a noisy, energetic city. It was still too new to boast many monuments, for it had been only five years since Philip II had moved the court to Madrid, which was then no more than a rustic country town. However, it rapidly spread out on both sides of the river Manzanares, and what it lacked in grandeur it made up for in animation. From earliest morning—for the Spaniards got up at dawn—people of every description crowded the colorful streets. Those who did not have horses or mules to ride—and excluding the ladies who were borne on litters by strong men—invaded the city on foot over unpaved streets whose sharp stones cut their feet. The space was shared by their domestic animals.

The fashions of the time enabled a newcomer to recognize at a glance the occupation of those he saw. For example, the physician wore a big stone ring, which, according to the satirist Quevedo, predicted the tomb which awaited anyone who entrusted himself to the doctor. The student was identified by his four-cornered academic cap and his trailing gown. The soldier, without a definite uniform, was recognized by the colored plumes on his hat and by his self-assured walk.

Now and then everyone hastened to watch a procession in which a woman, usually old, and naked from the waist up, would be riding on a donkey. She was considered a witch and she was publicly paying her debt to society for her evil works: for acting as a procuress, for casting the "evil eye" on persons, and for her supposedly frequent rendezvous with the Devil. The people demanded this kind of public punishment.

Many of them were going about their various jobs, but another, more numerous group had nothing better to do than to stroll about the city. These were known as *pretendientes*, or claimants. Generally they were former soldiers, who, having completed several years of service, believed that this was the moment for the King to reward them with some position or assignment that would permit them to live out their days with reasonable comfort and security.

They flocked to the capital, bearing documents and references that they presented to a secretary, and then waited about for what they had requested. They felt certain of being named to the posts they sought, convinced that it was fair that they should be. Unfortunately the hopefuls were many, and the bureaucracy of his Majesty was slow. Days passed into weeks, and still they waited for some confirmation which did not come. What else was there to do but spend their time hanging around the Palace, inquiring about the progress of their petitions, then wandering about the city, spending their meager economic resources?

It never occurred to most of these noble gentlemen to take advantage of the hours they were wasting by getting some remunerative work. For such *caballeros*, bearing arms was the only task for which they used their hands.

Also swelling the crowds on the streets were the servants

of large households. The haughtiness of the Spaniards was such that when a young man inherited his father's house, he did not dismiss those servants whom he did not need. After all, what would people say of a gentleman who was reduced to such economy? But since there was not enough work to keep them all busy, they were free to roam the streets or find themselves part-time jobs to round out their wages.

The important cities lured the *picaros*, or rogues, for wherever there was activity, there was money. These were usually young lads as ingenious as they were shameless. All of them—doctors, pompous soldiers, students—must have passed a thousand times the man who was later to portray them in his *Interludes, Exemplary Novels*, and in the pages of *Don Quixote*. Because in this year of 1566, mingling with Madrid's lively and motley crowds, observing all there was to see, listening to everything, making mental notes of witty remarks, turns of phrase, manners of walking and dressing, was a young man just nineteen years old. His name was Miguel de Cervantes Saavedra.

Cervantes was born in nearby Alcalá, a city of more tradition than the capital, having had a bishop and a university long before Madrid. His father was a surgeon, a profession distinguished from that of a doctor and signifying far less than it does now. Cervantes himself wrote in "The Divorce Court," one of his *Interludes*, about a wife who complains to a judge that she had been deceived into believing her husband was a doctor, but he turned out to be a surgeon, therefore worth half as much. His mission was to apply bandages, set broken bones, and practice bloodletting, either by leeches or by opening a vein with a lancet. Bleeding, known as the *sangría*, was the most common remedy used by the medical men of the time. They believed that they could cure anything by expelling some blood. They reasoned that the poison causing illness would thus flow out of the patient's body. One must add that life itself frequently was expelled along with the blood.

The family of Miguel de Cervantes provided him with a combination of positive and negative elements that were to accompany him all his life. From his father, a jovial and kindly man, he inherited the most valued possession in sixteenth-century Spain, which set such a premium on nobility: a name with no stigma of Moorish or Jewish blood. Those in whose veins flowed such "uncontaminated" blood were called "old Christians." It was an important factor, which, in principle at least, would permit Miguel to climb to fortune's heights.

Along with the good fortune of his lineage, Cervantes was blessed with a family who were frighteningly deficient in managing their finances. The young man heard mentioned often a word that was to plague him all his life— debts. He became well acquainted with men who called to collect money that did not exist; with threats of imprisonment of his father, which twice were fulfilled; with journeys hastily undertaken to escape creditors; with visits to relatives to beg help.

His sisters displayed the same combination of disorder and generosity. Doña Andrea was involved with a married man by whom she had a daughter. She accepted gifts from other men, all of which were accompanied by a great profusion of documents. These documents, of course, served to broadcast her indiscretions to the rest of the world. But this sister and the other one, Doña Magdalena, were to give up their dowries in order to ransom their brother from captivity in Algiers.

The mother of Cervantes, heaped with misfortunes, with endless debts, with the anxiety of seemingly endless moves, was the strength of the family. More aggressive than her inefficient husband, she declared herself a widow on more than one occasion, even while her husband lived, in order to evoke compassion from the government officials with whom she had to deal.

Perhaps the only member of the family who brought any measure of satisfaction to Miguel was his brother Rodrigo, three years his junior. For many years the two of them served in the military together and established a bond that was broken only by Rodrigo's death in battle at Flanders in 1600.

It was, then, a family good in intention, dismally lacking in economic organization, capable of indiscretions perhaps inspired more by poverty than anything else, and capable, too, of repentance. Independent in their caprices, they were united in their misfortunes. Stability was not one of their virtues. But the combination of goodness, lack of fiscal order, and bad luck often self-inflicted was to characterize Miguel de Cervantes himself.

Debts obliged the family of Don Rodrigo, the father, to leave Alcalá and to live in a constant state of flight from creditors, seeking out relatives who might give them refuge in Valladolid, Córdoba, Cabra, or Seville. Naturally this jeopardized the formal education of Miguel. (Records show that at nineteen years of age he was studying in Madrid courses which were normally passed at fifteen.) On the other hand, he did gain, from his earliest years, an impressive experience with life. The necessity of flight, the first-hand acquaintance with poverty became one with his memory of new landscapes and places, new types of persons seen and heard along the roads of Andalusia and La Mancha.

In 1568 Cervantes was still in Madrid, and to all appearances was there to stay. Wherever the capital, there was the activity. The important positions were to be found there, and most important, there dwelt possible benefactors or patrons of the arts. For by now Cervantes saw himself as a poet. His Latin teacher, López de Hoyos, distinguished him among his classmates by choosing one of his sonnets to be published. It was a poem commemorating the death of Isabella of Valois, wife of Philip II. Cervantes was sure he had found the direction his life was to take. Those small groups or cliques of people who had nothing to do would discuss his poems. They would be read in the literary academies. It was even possible that his fame would reach the ears of some nobleman who might offer him protection and generously reward him. The only thing the poet would have to do was to dedicate one of his poems to his benefactor. This was just what he had been waiting for.

These two aspirations of Cervantes seem unrelated to the reality of today, but at that time poetry was a route to fame, for the epoch was a poetic one. The Renaissance had thrust upon the world a cultural and literary zeal that recognized poetry as the queen of literary forms. Dramas were written in verse, and many literary figures corresponded with each other in verse. A man in love made sure that his first letter to his beloved was in rhyme. There were even instances of government affairs being negotiated in verse.

Patronage of the arts had returned, along with other

Roman customs, as an outcome of the Renaissance. A nobleman was happy to have his generosity praised by a humble poet's compositions. Today it seems strangely humiliating that a writer would lower his dignity to such a point, especially when we see on a title page the name of a brilliant author, joined with that of an aristocrat who never did anything of importance in his life. But that was the custom, and no writer felt it was degrading to ask for patronage from the one who had the most to give.

Cervantes felt he could write poetry. Perhaps later he would try his hand at writing plays, but for the moment it was enough for him that his name was beginning to be known. Slender, blond, with a slightly aquiline nose, the lad from Alcalá strolled about Madrid, full of life and interested in everything.

He had tasted his first triumph, which would also be his first failure. Cervantes was not to go down in history as a poet. It was the first shock of the many encounters with reality that he was to experience along the road of his illusions. The circumstances that made him detour from the route which was so much to his taste and in which he felt so sure of success came through an encounter with a builder assigned to the Royal Palaces.

The Spaniards of this period carried swords, probably as a habit left over from the days when constant struggle against the Moors required the Christians always to be prepared. By the time the Reconquest was concluded, the custom was too firmly entrenched to be suppressed. Usually the sword was worn on the left side and was considered part of a person's dress. A man placed his fingers on the hilt, his arm resting lightly on it, and the pressure raised the point and gave a flare to his cape. His right hand remained free to adjust his hat, play with the chain worn at the neck, or stroke his beard or mustache. Hands and legs, exposed, were a manifestation of masculine vanity and were supposed to attract feminine curiosity and admiration. All of the *hidalgos*, or noblemen, wore swords (those of lesser rank carried daggers), and these had to be of certain dimensions determined by law.

But what was the use of them? Duels had been definitively prohibited. King after king during the last years had threatened to punish severely anyone who used his sword to attack someone. The Spaniards read the orders that were posted on the street corners and kept right on doing as they pleased. Who among them was going to contain his anger or curb his eagerness to avenge himself just because some ruler from his dais had decided that sword play was evil?

It was a day in December of 1568. As usual the environs of the Royal Palace were alive with a mob of importunate gentlemen, accompanied by their servants. As secretaries emerged from their offices with an important air, the loafers, soliciting favors, pressed in upon them. Clerks and lawyers swarmed among the groups, cautioning, advising, raising the hopes of their clients by assuring them of success in their requests—as long as the gentlemen would advance a few escudos (money of the epoch) to carry on the petitions in their behalf.

Suddenly in the midst of the throng a woman screamed. The crowd pushed forward, and the palace guards hastened to see what had happened. A man named Antonio De Seguera lay bleeding on the ground. The police obtained testimony from all who were present and, when he was able to talk, from the victim himself. After a violent argument a duel had been fought. The aggressor? He had fled. Did the wounded man know him? Yes. His name was Miguel de Cervantes. He was from Alcalá, a student and something of a poet.

Through the side streets around the Palace the young man fled, his dreams of glory now turned into a single obsession—to run away as far as possible. He did not know in what condition he had left his opponent, whether or not he had killed him, but he had no desire whatever to face the King's magistrates. Prison or the gallows loomed before him, an end vastly different from what he had dreamed for himself as poet laureate.

The Cervantes admired as a poet, the man whose verses and clever sayings were beginning to be noticed, had suddenly become a delinquent. Even though he had wounded his opponent according to the rules of dueling, the law would not accept this. Besides, the incident had occurred on the grounds of the Royal Palace. His disobedience of the law thus seemed tinged with sacrilege, for he had shown lack of respect to him who, after God, was most important to Spaniards—His Majesty, the King.

Cervantes went into hiding. The news that reached him confirmed his worst fears. Indeed, the scene of his crime had made the judges more than usually severe. The sentence demanded that "his right hand be cut off in public—*con vergüenza pública*—ten years of exile from the capital, and other penalties."

Con vergüenza pública. That meant exposure to the curiosity and mockery of the people. For a Spaniard who laid claims to nobility, as did Cervantes, this was a grave injury. And what was more, the right hand—the hand of the sword and of the pen!

Cervantes did not resign himself to such punishment. By devious routes at night the young man from Alcalá fled in order to save his hand and his dignity. Keeping out of sight of the Holy Brotherhood, who policed the highways and countryside in those days, he left for Valencia, then proceeded along the coast to Barcelona. Here he was safe, for although the King was the same, Castilian law was not in effect in Aragon or in Catalonia, where they had their own special laws known then as *fueros*.

Looking out upon the Mediterranean, Cervantes felt free and contented. Perhaps it was this sensation of freedom, this opportunity to catch his breath after his recent anxieties that inspired him to dedicate to the city of Barcelona one of the finest eulogies ever to come from his pen:

"Barcelona, archive of courtesy, refuge of foreigners, asylum of the poor, fatherland of the brave, revenge of the offended, home of firm friendships, and in location and beauty, unique."

On the other side of that blue sea was Italy, which in the sixteenth century held an enormous attraction for any Spaniard with an itch to travel. Ever since that country had become a battlefield in the conflict between France and Spain, the names of Naples, Rome, and Palermo were as familiar to the Spaniard as his own Valencia and Valladolid. The beauty of the landscape, the charm of the people, and the gentle climate had occasioned for the Spanish soldier some verses that reflected what he could expect in the battlefield:

> España mi natura;
> Italia mi ventura;
> Flandes mi sepultura.

They lose their grace in translation, but the idea is:

> In Spain my nature;
> In Italy my happiness;
> In Flanders my grave.

For in Flanders the sun became mist. The luminosity of Italy changed to dismal gloom, and the cheerful campaign became an inferno against enemies who fiercely fought for their independence and for their Protestant faith against the Catholic Spaniard.

Cervantes' own love of Italy was colored by his literary interests. The Renaissance which was then invading Spain had originated in Italy; from Italy came the sonnet, the literary form to which Cervantes was so addicted; from Italy, too, had come the cult of Greek and Roman civilizations which had so influenced the Renaissance.

Without further thought, Cervantes took a definitive step in his life. He crossed the Alps. (Ten months later— His Majesty's justice was slow but sure—he was judged guilty of rebellion and an order was sent out to arrest him wherever he might be found.)

His first experience of Italy was Genoa. Years later he was to remember with pleasure his impressions of this and other Italian cities and describe them in *The Man of Glass*. Of Genoa he writes, in the character of Tomás, that he

. . . admired the blond hair of the Genoese girls, and the charming and gallant disposition of the men, the admirable beauty of the city, with its houses set high in the cliffs, resembling diamonds mounted in gold.

A feeling for the extent of his travels is given in this passage:

The following day all the companies . . . going to Piedmont disembarked, but Tomás did not care to make that journey, preferring to go by land from Genoa by way of Rome and Naples, intending to return by the magnificent city of Venice, and by Loretto to Milan and Piedmont, where Don Diego de Valdivia said they would meet if he and his men had not already been sent off to Flanders as they all expected.

Cervantes writes that Tomás visited Lucca and then Florence:

He was delighted with Florence because of its pleasant setting, cleanliness, magnificent buildings, cool river, and calm streets. He spent four days there, then left for Rome, the queen of cities and mistress of the world. He visited her temples, worshipped her relics, and admired her grandeur.

Rome! This was the classic beauty that the Popes, so greatly enamored of antiquity, were striving to dig up and display. They were in the process of finishing the gigantic basilica of St. Peter. Luxury and vice. The cardinals rivaled the princes in elegance.

Cervantes approached one of them, Cardinal Acquaviva, who had earlier been a special envoy of the Pope to Madrid. The cardinal took this bright young man into his household as a *criado* (not exactly a servant but in the capacity of secretary or assistant), a position much sought after by young men of good families. It was a pleasant situation which promised a certain economic security, and the work left enough free time in which to write and to stroll through the Via Giulia, which Pope Julius II had built with taxes paid by the prostitutes of Rome.

Cervantes visited the marketplace at Campo dei Fiori, where just about everything was bought and sold. From St. Peter's dome, whose construction had been directed by Michelangelo, he saw nearby Adriana and the Castle of Saint Angelo, where the Pope had taken refuge when the Spanish attacked Rome in 1527.

Never had there been a more intense, a more international, or livelier city. But the gentle murmur of gaiety and opulence was at times drowned out by a faint rumbling from the east. When this was perceived in the streets of Rome, the cardinal left the palace, the courtesan abandoned her business, and the diplomat laid down his pen. It was the beginning of a storm that could demolish all of that wealth. It was a wind blowing from Constantinople.

In the seventh century Mohammed, a man born to be a leader, lighted a bonfire by founding the Islamic religion, which included missionary endeavor and conversion among its principles. Mohammed instilled in the nomadic, war-oriented man of the desert a reason for his existence. He convinced him to sublimate his warlike instincts into religious zeal. There was only one god, Allah, and Mohammed was his prophet. All those who opposed this would be fought against as infidels. Those who accepted the Islamic faith and were converted would be considered as brothers. Those who surrendered could continue to practice their own religion by paying a tax to the Moslems.

The Islamic religion is uncomplicated.[1] The Moslems believe in one God and pray facing the holy city of Mecca. It is comprehensive: A man may have four legal wives and as many concubines as he can support. It is hygienic: They abstain from pork and practice ablutions.

In ten years, 622–632, the Islamic faith, from its base in Arabia, shot out like a flame throughout all of the coast of North Africa on the one side and through Asia Minor on the other. It included racially distinct groups of people: Egyptians, Berbers, Algerians, Persians, Syrians. However, the belief common to all of them was that Islam meant salvation. On a map, Islam has the shape of a crescent, the right tip nailed in front of Constantinople where the Byzantine empire, successor to the Roman, held the Islamic offensive in check for eight centuries. But, in the other direction, it rapidly spread along the African coast, jumped over into Spain, easily conquering the Visigoths then in power on the peninsula.

It passed through the Pyrenees, entering into France. In a few years after the death of Mohammed, his followers were already near the center of Europe. The French king, Charles Martel, stopped the offensive in Poitiers in 732, but the Moslems remained in Spain for nearly eight centuries. Before they were expelled in 1492 they had finally succeeded in breaking down the other front. (Constantinople, the doorway to Europe, fell in 1453.) In 1553, the Moslem Turks were facing Vienna. (One must note the short distance between Poitiers and Vienna.) Only the lack of historical coordination between these two points of the Islamic offensive kept the whole of Europe from prostrating itself, facing Mecca.

In 1570, when Cervantes was in Italy, the Moslem danger still existed, as it had throughout the Middle Ages. Only now it was called the Turkish menace. From Constantinople, Sultan Selim II dominated all of eastern Europe. Budapest, Sofia, and Athens were his, and through his subordinates, the coast of North Africa. Selim could, when he felt like it, declare a large-scale war. But the small wars never ceased, not even for a moment.

From Oran in Algeria, small swift ships known as galliots continually attacked the coasts of Spain and Italy. In these rapid raids the Turks would disembark, taking their victims by surprise, killing the men, and holding the women and children as captives. The women were added to their harems and the boys to the Turkish army. They robbed and pillaged, and by the time hastily assembled troops reached the scene, the enemy was already on the high seas with his booty. This was the usual pattern.

Today along the coasts of Majorca, Catalonia, and Valencia, one can still see the towers or lookouts where watchmen used to scrutinize the horizon, ever ready to ring bells and light fires to alert the people to an imminent attack. One can still note on the Catalonian and Majorcan coasts towns of the same name: Arenys de Munt and Arenys de Mar (Arenys on the Mountain and Arenys on the Sea), Soller and the port of Soller, Manacor and the port of Manacor.

All of the Christian countries were suffering from a psychosis of fear in 1570. Selim II had at various times announced his intention to deal the death blow to Christianity. Rumors were rampant. Was he preparing an army? Was he recruiting troops? Spies came and went with their reports. Apart from those who managed to get inside Constantinople, there were some who ventured in light vessels along the Turkish-occupied coasts in order to count the enemy ships and by studying the preparations they were making, get some idea of their readiness for an offensive.

In the second part of *Don Quixote,* when the household is trying to attest to the recovery of the knight's sanity, we find an allusion to this constant fear:

The curate changed his original plan, which was not to touch on the subject of chivalry, and decided to thoroughly test Don Quixote's recovery to see if it were genuine or false, so talking of one thing and then another, he finally mentioned some news that had come from the capital, and among other things, he said that it was certain that the Turks were descending with a powerful fleet, but no one knew their plans nor where such a mighty storm would break.

Because of this fear, which almost every year calls us to arms, all Christendom was alerted, and His Majesty had made provisions for the defense of the coast of Naples, Sicily and the island of Malta.

The preoccupation was no more than natural. In the face of such power, wealth, and Turkish fanaticism, the Christian powers could depend for sure on but two defenders —Spain and the Pope. Although they were united by the same religion, they were much less in accord politically. The Pope, of course, wanted Spain to be stronger than the Turks, but not so powerful that she could dominate all of Italy and the Pope as well. This situation kept France, the other Mediterranean power, from aiding Spain at all, since they were rivals for leadership. France, a Christian country, remained neutral. There remained only one possible ally—Venice, an exception in the ideological dispute.

A commercial power, Venice, until then, had never encountered difficulty in trading with any people known at that time, including the Turks themselves. The idea of a military alliance with such diametric opposites as the

Papal government and Spain was not in any way attractive to Venice.

Or at least not until the Turk forgot or ignored his mercantile association with the Republic of Venice, and attacked one of her possessions, the island of Cyprus.

THE SOLDIER

The ambassadors of the Most Serene Republic, as Venice was known, became alarmed. Urgent messages came and went between Venice, Rome, and Madrid. While mutual distrust delayed any agreement, Famagusta, the capital of Cyprus, fell to the Turks, and its defender, Bragadino, was impaled. A wave of indignation and fear swept through the Western World. Former differences were forgotten, for now they had to hold back the Turkish offensive at whatever cost. So one spring day in 1571 the Holy League was formed among the Papacy, the King of Spain, the Republic of Venice, and the Order of Malta. They were still not certain as to who would head the coalition. Venice claimed it should be a Venetian because of her greater experience as a maritime power. Spain countered that it was she who furnished the most troops and ships. The King of Spain was to name the commander-in-chief of the fleet. He chose his half brother, Don Juan of Austria, the natural son of Charles V. A handsome and valiant young man, he was known as captain-general.

Preparations were being made and an adventurous air was blowing through Italy. Music of military bands accompanied the recruiting officers calling for men to enlist. Cervantes describes such a scene in *The Man of Glass*, when the hero chances to meet a gentleman on horseback:

. . . He joined him and they became traveling companions. They chatted on various topics, and in short time Tomás revealed his rare intelligence, and the gentleman gave evidence of his gallantry and good breeding. The latter said that he was an infantry captain in His Majesty's service. . . .

He praised to the skies the freedom of the soldier's life in Italy, but said not a word about the chilling cold of sentry duty, the dangers of raids, the terrors of battles, the hunger endured in a siege, the destruction caused by mines, or other such matters, although there are some who consider these weary aspects of the military life as its principal characteristic. In short, he talked so long and so well that Tomás Rodaja's natural judgment began to waver, and he felt attracted to that way of life which is always so near death.

The captain, whose name was Don Diego Valdiva, was highly pleased with the good looks, lively intelligence, and manners of Tomás, and invited him to accompany him to Italy if he was curious to see the country. He offered to share his mess with him, and if necessary, his flag, because his [own] ensign was to leave him shortly.

Tomás did not need much encouragement to accept the captain's invitation, for he quickly reflected that it would be a fine idea to see Italy and Flanders and other countries, since extensive travel makes one wise. At most, this would require but three or four years, and since he was young, there would be nothing to keep him from returning to his studies afterward. . . .

They reached Antequera that night and in a few days, by traveling great distances, they overtook the recently recruited company, and with four others, began the march to Cartagena, lodging at any place they happened to find along the way.

Now Tomás had a chance to observe the authority flouted by the commissaries, the inflexibility of some of the captains, the greediness of the quartermasters, the manner in which the paymasters kept their accounts, the complaints of the recruits, the quarrels of the guests of the inns, the requests for more supplies than necessary, and finally the unavoidable necessity of doing all that he had observed and which appeared to him to be bad.

Having discarded his student costume, Tomás had dressed

himself up in gaudy colors and assumed the swaggering airs of a veteran soldier.

Farewell to the sane and well-organized position in the palace of Cardinal Acquaviva. Cervantes, accompanied in his undertaking by his brother Rodrigo, who had left Spain in search of adventure, donned his bright-colored Spanish soldier's uniform, which was so extreme that the Italians called it *papagallo* (parrot). He entered into the usual diversions that make up the life of the soldier in an occupied country.

In the gay and bustling city of Naples, Cervantes fell in love with a girl called Silena, and from that affair had a son whom he named Promontorio. Years later the writer was to refer to him with much nostalgia, as if the memory of him represented the happiness of those years. Never had Cervantes felt more carefree. At twenty-four he enjoyed that life which, on the one hand, gave him such pleasures, and on the other, brought him the feeling of performing his duty in the service of his king against the enemy, the Turk, and in the service of the Church against the enemy Mohammed.

The regiment of Naples was, according to military organization of the time, an infantry division. Naval strategy had not yet reached the point of staging an artillery duel, which is the principal characteristic of sea battles today. Until well into the sixteenth century, a land concept of battle was maintained, and the function of the ships was to approach the enemy vessel; the infantry would seize it with grappling irons, then jump on board, fighting hand to hand with sword and pike. That is why ships used to carry such large contingents of men and relatively few cannons.

Finally the preparations were complete, the fleets were assembled and they sailed out to face the enemy. There were 208 galleys, 6 galleasses, 57 frigates, and various small liaison boats. The instructions of the King to Don Juan of Austria had been typical of one who felt the mission was as much religious as political. The soldiers and sailors, under penalty of death, were prohibited from swearing. Gambling was forbidden. There were the customary bickerings among the allies. A Venetian captain hanged a Spaniard who had been insolent to him, and the companions of the dead soldier threatened to attack the ships of the Venetian Republic. Don Juan of Austria intervened and pacified everyone. It was necessary to maintain a unified fleet to face the enemy.

The Turks promptly appeared along the Greek coast in the Gulf of Lepanto. The reports of his force had not been exaggerated. A gigantic fleet advanced in the formation of a half moon, the Moslem symbol, toward that of the allied forces of the Holy League. Don Juan of Austria directed his fleet in the form of a wedge. The Turks intended to surround the Christians, while the latter meant to break the enemy formation and then finish off the resultant isolated groups. The Venetian, Barbarigo, advised Don Juan of Austria to cut the rams of the galleys. In this way the flotation line would be lower and shots from enemy cannons, aimed at the gunwale, would pass over the deck. And so it was done. Then the commander of the fleet passed quickly in front of his ships. With the banner of the Holy League in his hand, he exhorted the soldiers and sailors to fight to their utmost.

The galleasses fired their first cannon shots and retired to the rear guard. Other ships increased their speed. Christians found themselves on Turkish galleys, and Turks or galley slaves who paid for their guilt on Christian galleys bent over the oars while the boatswain drove them by his gestures and voice, and if necessary, with the whip. They resembled arrows crossing the sea until they nailed themselves onto an enemy ship.

Don Quixote, delivering a discourse on arms and letters, speaks of the fear of a soldier who knows that the enemy is about to blow up the place where he stands guard. He goes on to say:

And if this be thought small danger, let us see if it is equaled or surpassed by the collision of two galleys, prow to prow, in mid-ocean, both of them pinned and grappled together, leaving the soldier no more space than two feet of plank at the ram to stand upon. With all of this he sees in front of him as many ministers of death . . . as there are cannons of the artillery aimed at him from the enemy vessel, no farther from his body than the length of a lance. And though he sees that the slightest slip of his foot would send him to the depths of Neptune, nevertheless with intrepid heart and inspired by the honor which drives him, he lets himself be the target for so many muskets and tries to force his way along that narrow passageway on to the enemy's ship. And what is most to be admired is that scarcely had one fallen never to rise again when another takes his place; and if he too falls into the sea, which like an enemy awaits him, another and yet another succeeds him with no time at all between their deaths. In all of the hazards of war there is no greater courage and daring than this.

This description of a soldier's experience in sea fighting comes from Cervantes' memory of his own gallant behavior during "the greatest event of the centuries," the famous battle of Lepanto, in 1571. The shouting and uproar of the troops wakened him from his lethargy, for he was sick with a fever, probably typhoid, but he staggered up on deck where his captain ordered him to go back down, for he considered him too sick to fight. Cervantes persisted. He preferred to die in the open air and fighting. Simple young soldier that he was, he so impressed the captain that the latter gave him command of a skiff and twelve men of his galley, *Marquesa*. When the fighting was over, Cervantes had been wounded twice in the chest and a third bullet had deprived him of the use of his left hand for the rest of his life.

The Christians were the victors in this battle. Alí Baja, commander of the Turkish fleet, was strung up on a pike to impress both friends and enemies. The left wing of the Turkish fleet, along with its commanding officer "Tiñoso," escaped the disaster and went back to report the defeat to their infuriated Sultan. By nightfall the Christian fleet was counting its own dead and those of the enemy floating upon the sea. (According to a popular belief, Christian bodies floated face up, while those of the Mohammedan faith floated face down.)

A triumphal welcome awaited their return to Messina. For a young man of twenty-four, what could possibly surpass returning as a hero, and as a wounded hero at that? Admiral Don Juan of Austria greeted the soldiers lying on their crude cots. He rewarded Cervantes with a medal for bravery. And Cervantes? His fever was nearly gone and his wounds were healing. What greater satisfaction could he imagine? The news of the triumphant battle circulated throughout the entire Christian world, and all of those who had taken part in it knew they could proudly say, "I was there." It was unnecessary to designate it by the name Lepanto. It sufficed merely to mention "sea battle" for the listener to know that one was referring to that great day when the enemy of the Western World had his wings clipped.

But coalitions, especially those forced by circumstances, last about as long as the sensation of the victory itself. Once the enemy is destroyed and no longer presents a danger, national egos again come to the surface. Venice, the day following the victory, was resistant to new adventures. She would rather have resumed her friendly trade relations with the Turks. Nor was Philip II overly inclined to further exalt the glory of the hero of the day, Don Juan of Austria, because he distrusted his youthful ambition. So what could have been the death blow to the Turk was limited to a series of not too significant enterprises.

Disillusion was widespread. Cervantes describes these futile days to us in the *Quixote*:

. . . I found myself the second year, which was seventy-two, at Navarino rowing in the admiral's galley. I saw and made note of how the opportunity of capturing the entire Turkish fleet in that harbor was lost. All of the sailors and Janissaries[2] aboard were so certain they would be attacked in that port that they had at hand their clothes and *pasamaques*, which were their shoes, ready to flee at once by land without waiting to be attacked, so great was their fear of our fleet. But fate ordered it otherwise, not through any fault or neglect of our general, but for the sins of Christendom and because it is God's will that we are always punished. In the end, Aluch Alí took Modoń, which is an island near Navarino, and throwing his men ashore, he fortified the mouth of the harbor and remained quiet until Don Juan turned back.

During this expedition, the galley called *The Prize* was taken. Her captain was the son of that famous corsair Barbarossa. It was taken by the flag ship of Naples, called *The*

She-Wolf, commanded by that thunderbolt of war, by that father to his soldiers, by that fortunate, unbeaten captain, Don Alvaro de Bazán, Marquis of Santa Cruz. . . .

We returned to Constantinople the following year, which was '73, where it became known that Don Juan had seized Tunis, and taking that kingdom from the Turks, placed it in the possession of Muley Hamet, thus dashing the hopes which Muley Hamida, the cruelest and bravest Moor in the world, nurtured of regaining rule. The Grand Turk greatly felt this loss, and employing the shrewdness inherent in his race, he made peace with the Venetians, who desired it much more than he, and in the following year of '74, he attacked the Goleta and the fort that Don Juan had left half built near Tunis. While all of these events took place, I was drudging away at the oars, rowing and rowing with no hope whatever of freedom. At any rate, I had no hopes of obtaining my liberty by ransom because I was determined not to write to my father the news of my misfortunes. . . .

In a sonnet at the beginning of Chapter 40 of the *Quixote*, Cervantes laments the defeat of Tunis so soon after the victory of Lepanto. He praises the valor of the three thousand soldiers who fell on the barren, battle-ridden sands of Tunis, a land whose tragic memories have haunted the Spaniard for centuries. He says there have been none braver than these men whose saintly souls have flown to their heavenly abode, but that the struggle was in vain.

Cervantes spent the years 1571 to 1574 in military service, which at that time he was probably hoping to make his career. Encouraged by his initial success, delighted by the beauty of the Italian cities as well as by the women of that country, what more could he wish?

He resumed his affair with Silena, which he had begun

before Lepanto. This love and the endearments of their son Promontorio were a great pleasure to him. Indeed, it is quite possible that Cervantes felt inclined to some sort of permanence in this pleasant situation. However, the military profession beckoned him. After all, as his alter ego, Don Quixote, said, arms offered a great deal more to a man than a literary career:

Away with those who would say letters are preferable to arms; I will tell them, whoever they may be, that they don't know what they are talking about. The reason they usually give and to which they hold is that labors of the mind are superior to those of the body and that arms are exercised by the body alone as though it were the business of porters, which required nothing more than physical strength; or as if that which we term the profession of arms did not demand acts of fortitude which depend upon a high degree of intelligence. . . .

These, then, I tell you, are the hardships a student endures: first, poverty (not that all are poor, but I wish to state the case as strongly as possible), and having said that he suffers poverty, it seems to me there is little more to say of his misery, for he who is poor is lacking in every comfort. He suffers poverty in all of its parts: hunger, cold, nakedness, or in a combination of all of it. But, everything considered, he does eat, even though it may be somewhat later than the usual hour, and although it may consist of scraps from the table of the rich or perhaps by the humiliation of begging soup at the convent doors. Nor do they fail to run onto a brazier or fireplace in someone's house, where, if they do not warm themselves, they at least dispel a little of the cold and sleep under cover. . . .

Now tell me, gentlemen, if you have ever thought about it, how many less are those who have been rewarded by war than those who have perished in it? No doubt you will reply that there is no comparison. The dead cannot be counted, while those who survive to receive rewards number less than a thousand. The opposite is true with scholars. Their salary and other remunerations furnish them a livelihood. Therefore, though the soldier's reward is less, his labors are greater. One can answer that it is easier to reward two thousand scholars than thirty thousand soldiers, because the former are rewarded by employments, which of necessity are given to those of their profession, while the latter can only be remunerated from the property of the master they serve, and this impossibility only strengthens my argument. But let us leave this question aside, for it is too difficult to resolve, and return to the superiority of arms over letters. It is said in support of letters that arms could not exist without them, for war also has its laws to which it is subject, and laws fall in the realm of scholars. Those in favor of arms will reply to this that without them laws could not be enforced because it is by arms that republics are defended, kingdoms are preserved, cities are protected, roads are made safe, and the seas kept free of pirates. In short, if it were not for arms, countries, kingdoms, monarchies, cities, seaways and highways would be subject to the ravages and confusion which accompanies war for its duration, and is free to use its privileges and powers.

It is a fact that what costs most is and should be most esteemed. To attain eminence in letters costs a man time, periods of hunger, nakedness, dizziness in the head, indigestion and other vexations to which I have already referred. But to gradually become a good soldier requires of one everything that it costs the student, but in such a greater degree that there is no comparison, because at every moment he is in danger of losing his life.

Cervantes seemed convinced of the superiority of a military career. He asked for a commission as ensign, which was not granted, perhaps because of the paralysis of his left hand; an officer needs two hands in combat. Once more destiny cut short the route he thought he saw so clearly. After one success he had to change his direction and look for something else.

But what? Like thousands of his countrymen he would utilize his military reputation to secure a government job. A post in America, perhaps as governor of some stronghold. His record was brilliant, so who would refuse him that which he rightly had coming to him? Besides, his return to Madrid was now possible. As was the custom in those times, his parents had managed, by a cash settlement, to get the offended and wounded Antonio de Siguera (now a brilliant overseer of the Royal Palaces of Madrid and Aranjuez) to withdraw his case against Cervantes. The judge, in view of this, revoked the sentence. Miguel could return to the capital whenever he liked, where surely a recompense awaited him in return for his years of service to the king.

In order to achieve anything in Spain, he would need, then as now, more than just permission to return, and that was a letter of recommendation. Four years had passed since Lepanto and the memory of man is short. Would anyone grant him this?

His apprehensions were groundless. Don Juan of Austria, the commander-in-chief of the allied forces, wrote a glowing letter of praise for him. Other officers under whom he served also wrote laudatory letters describing the heroic deeds of this native of Alcalá, extolling his qualities of leadership and the nobility of his actions.

And so it appeared certain to Cervantes that he was to find in Madrid a situation commensurate with his worth. Besides, he was looking forward to a warm reunion with his mother and father and sisters and brothers, whom he had not seen in years. With his letters of recommendation zealously guarded in a tube made of tin, he began preparations for the trip home. His brother Rodrigo was to accompany him, and they would have to take great precautions not to ruin the occasion by falling victim to the typical danger of the western Mediterranean—Algerian pirates. Therefore Cervantes waited for the opportune moment. He knew it was better to calm his impatience to get home and wait until several galleys could travel together, helping each other should it be necessary.

Finally in September of 1575, such an expedition was ready to sail. It consisted of three well-armed galleys able to defend themselves against whatever danger. The pirates usually sailed in some nondescript vessel, because the entire secret of their success was the element of surprise, and this was a way to assure it.

The flotilla sailed out of the harbor and skirted along the coast of France for greater security. But often in September the Gulf of Lions offers disagreeable surprises. A storm dispersed the flotilla. The three vessels that were to have navigated together were separated, each one attempting to ride out the storm as best it could. In the one named *The Sun* the two Cervantes brothers feverishly helped the sailors. The storm subsided, but there was no trace of the other two ships. Instead they were rapidly being closed in upon by three ships, and no scrutiny was needed to see that they were the dreaded enemy.

Their prows collided brutally against the side of *The Sun*. The Berbers jumped on board and everywhere arms clashed. The resistance of the Spaniards was violent, but they had no recourse except to surrender.

The Algerians, satisfied, had begun the preparations for

returning home with their prisoners and their captured vessel when suddenly they saw the silhouettes of the two other ships. The two galleys, separated from *The Sun* because of the storm, were hastening to rescue their sister ship. The corsairs knew they could not escape the Spaniards if they had to tow the captured galley, so they abandoned the ship, but not the prisoners, who were tied and thrown on the deck of the Algerian vessel. From where he lay, Cervantes could see the rescue ships coming toward them, but now too late. Traveling at full speed, the agile Algerians were rapidly heading south.

The Christian galleys could do nothing but watch them disappear into the distance. The only thing left to their captains was to prepare the notice which they would present upon their arrival in port: "The crew and complement of the galley, *The Sun*, has been lost. The ship has been recovered for His Majesty's service."

Years later Cervantes would remember that heartbreaking episode, and although exaggerating the number of enemy ships, which in reality were but three, he somehow justifies his misfortune in the pages of *La Galatea*:

The enemies were not long in coming, and the wind even less in calming down, which was the total cause of our undoing. They did not dare come on board, because seeing that the wind had died down, it seemed to them preferable to wait until daybreak to attack us. So they waited. By now we had counted them and realized that there were fifteen sturdy vessels surrounding us. At that moment our worst fears were confirmed as to our ruin. Even so, our valiant captain did not lose heart, nor did any of his men, but waited to see what the enemy would do.

Now that it was day, the flagship sent a renegade in a skiff to demand our captain to surrender. Seeing that it was obviously impossible for the Christians to defend themselves against so many vessels, which besides were Algiers' best, the renegade shouted to them that if his men fired, his general, Arnaute Mami, would hang him from the yardarm. With this and other threats he tried to persuade the Spanish captain to yield. But the latter refused and replied that if he did not leave at once, his cannons would sink him.

Upon hearing this reply, Arnaute saw to it that his ship was armed throughout, and began firing with such crashing speed and fury that it was a marvel. Our ship began to do the same, and accompanied with such good luck that a bullet aimed at an enemy ship who was firing on us from the stern, hit her near the harpings in such a way that, with no help forthcoming, it was soon swallowed up by the sea. When the Turks saw this they intensified their fighting and in four hours they had attacked us four times, and had retreated as many times, with much damage to themselves and no small amount to us.

But I don't want to weary you with all the details of this combat, so I will say no more except that after having fought sixteen hours, and after our captain and everyone else on board had been killed, after the ninth and final attack upon us, the enemies furiously came on board our ship. . . .

It was in this manner, without my having regained consciousness whatever, that they carried me onto the enemy flagship, where my wounds were cared for and cured with some diligence.

THE PRISONER

Algiers today is still a luminous city of violent contrasts —noisy and excitable amid the din of street vendors and buyers; serene behind hidden patios with playing fountains, the symbol of abundance to the man of the desert.

In the sixteenth century Algiers had the role of a border country and springboard. Politically dependent upon far-off Constantinople, her function was to serve the interests of the sultan. On the other hand, her nearness to the Christian world made Algiers suitable for the necessary political contacts with countries such as France, who often forsook her Christian principles for anti-Spanish sentiments. As a springboard for the Mohammedan forces, Algiers held an incalculable advantage. It was from her shores that most of the expeditions set forth to attack the towns along the Spanish or Italian coastlines.

The prisoners seized on these raids were valuable to the Algerians in various ways. They furnished motive power for the galleys. Ships still could not rely too much on the sails to move them, so then, as in Roman times, they were dependent upon the combined forces of a few dozen men chained to their rowing benches, bending forward and backward to the rhythm of the commands shouted at them by the boatswain. Later, Góngora, the great Spanish poet, composed a ballad that sings of these galley slaves, the sadness of their exile, and their enforced labor. The little that they were given to eat and the harsh treatment they received caused the death of many, but, incredibly, men of that time, so much more accustomed to hardship than those of today, were capable of spending five or six years at the oars and then resuming a normal life when they were fortunate enough to be freed by their Christian friends. Then they reversed roles; the sailors took their turn rowing and the former captives commanded them.

A prisoner also had commercial value. The new masters lost no time in seeing that news of a capture reached the family of the victim, so that they could do everything possible to raise money for his ransom. When the ransom money had been collected, it was entrusted to Trinitarian or Mercedarian friars, who, in spite of the double symbol of hate—Spanish and religious—which they must have represented to the Algerians, were amicably received in Algeria when they arrived on their charitable mission. Once there, they would begin to discuss the monetary aspects of the bargain, and if they reached an agreement, the prisoner would be freed and could return to Spain on the ship of some neutral power, such as Greece or Albania, or on a Spanish vessel which had permission to dock at Algiers. The fierce war being waged between Spaniards and Moors did not prevent arrangements that were beneficial to both sides.

The fate of the women who were kidnaped on the raids along the Spanish coast was something else. The young and beautiful ones were taken to the sultan's harem or to the harems of important dignitaries of Constantinople. It was practically impossible to ransom the children. Educated in Algiers or Turkey, they forgot their religion as they became Mohammedan converts. Thus Islam gained new followers and more soldiers for the future. Since religion was so important to the Moslems, conversion to their faith meant freedom for the adult captives. So it was natural that some of the more desperate or ambitious fell into the temptation. These renegades became noted for their ferocity and bravery against their fellow Spaniards, and for a logical reason: they knew that, if captured, they would not be pardoned, and so they fought with the desperation of men who had no other recourse.

Miguel de Cervantes had considered himself fortunate to have obtained so many brilliant letters of recommendation upon leaving Italy. But as usual in his life, this seeming luck brought him only misfortune. His captors were dazzled before so much praise. "This man," they said, "must be a great leader in his country," and they automatically increased the amount of the ransom they figured they could ask, until finally they fixed it at the then-fabulous sum of five hundred escudos. Cervantes protested that he was from a poor family whose members could never raise such an amount. But it was useless.

Perhaps that imagined importance, or the fact that he had a paralyzed hand, saved him from the hard toil of rowing. Cervantes became a *criado*. But the title did not represent, as it had with Cardinal Acquavia, a secretary or a person in a position of confidence. In this case, the *criado* was a slave who took care of the worst of the household chores and in payment was shouted at and pushed about. When he went into the street to fetch the water and other necessities, he was subject to the insults and derision of the children who made fun of the *Rumi* (Christian) and threw stones at him.

The following declaration was sworn to by Rodrigo de Chaves before a notary years later:

. . . likewise this witness knows because he was in contact with the said Miguel de Cervantes as a friend, that the said Miguel de Cervantes was in debt more than a thousand reales, which some Christian merchants who frequented the aforementioned city had lent him for food and other necessaries during his captivity, because the Moor who held him captive did not feed him during the entire time he was a prisoner. This is attested to by one who personally saw him and who was also a captive, as was the above-named Cervantes, and this is the truth, sworn to and witnessed and signed in his name.

A cold and official document to place Cervantes' debts on records. What tragedy lies in the words "because the Moor who held him captive did not feed him." Loss of freedom and the hardship of enforced labor were not enough. He had to beg, besides, from friends or passers-by a few coins for the mouthful of bread that his cruel master denied him.

That master, whose name was Dali Mimmi, felt for his captive a hatred tinged with admiration. He treated him badly, but he did not get rid of him. There was something in Cervantes' looks and in his self-assurance that fascinated Dali Mimmi. His intuition told him that here was a person different from the rest, but he believed it was due solely to higher social status. The confiscated letters only confirmed this judgment. Dali Mimmi treated Cervantes harshly because he wanted to subdue the pride of this young man from Alcalá. But he did not kill him as he had done with so many rebellious slaves, in part because he did not want to lose the fabulous ransom he hoped to obtain, and in part because there was something about this particular slave which, at the last minute, always held his anger in check.

Nevertheless, if ever in the history of captivity there was

someone who merited the ultimate punishment, it was Miguel de Cervantes. When he found out about the high price put upon him by his captors, he thought he would never be ransomed. He knew the financial condition of his family too well to entertain any illusions that they could pay the ransom, so he concluded that there was only one road open to him—escape.

In the history of Algiers few had accomplished such a thing. Ships were constantly coming and going in the port, and when they tied up there, the oars were carried ashore and stored so that the Christian galley slaves would not make a desperate attempt to get away. By land one would have to travel over miles of desert before reaching a Christian fortress; and the Moslem peasants were very happy if they could return a fugitive, thus serving both their god Mohammed and their pocket—for there was a reward offered to anyone handing over a slave.

None of these dangers seemed to overly impress Cervantes. Much in the same way that he had assumed command of a dozen soldiers at Lepanto when he had held no rank, now as leader among the captives of Algiers he outlined an escape which would have to be prepared with the utmost caution if they were to carry it out. He had been a prisoner only a few months, but already that was too long.

He assembled his friends, and they bought the services of a Moorish guide. One day, taking advantage of the relative liberty in which they were left to roam around the city while performing their duties as slaves, twelve of them met with their guide, who led them westward in the direction of Oran and freedom. But after a short while the Moor began to retrace his steps. He told them to wait, and then he disappeared. Perhaps he did not really know the road, or perhaps he feared the consequences of his act. The slaves discussed the possibility of continuing without him but could not agree. Without a guide they would have little chance of success. So the Christians returned, downcast, to their captivity.

Their situation naturally was harder now because of their audacity. Their work no longer consisted of fetching provisions and cleaning the house of the slave driver. They were always in chains, and they left their dungeon only to work with construction crews fortifying the port walls against attack by the Christians.

Meanwhile, in far away Madrid, the Cervantes family was frantically striving to accumulate enough funds to buy Miguel's liberty. They sold what little they had, then went to the *Consejo de la Cruzade* (Crusade Council) seeking financial help to save the son who had so bravely served his country and monarch. Cervantes' mother, in her petition, said she was a widow, a merciful lie invented to inspire compassion from the government and, indirectly, affirm the true state of the family, caused by the ineffectiveness of the father at its head. Finally, between the sale of their modest goods and loans, they collected a little money which they entrusted to some Redemptorist friars, who took it to Algiers.

Then, as in the sale of a horse, the bargaining began. The seller, Dali Mimmi, extolled the quality of his product —the nobility of his ancestry, his military bravery, his capacity to work. The buyers (the friars) tried to understate these values. In the case of Miguel de Cervantes, however, the disparity was excessive. Dali Mimmi laughed at the sum offered for his captive. He would not hand him over for less than five hundred escudos in gold. And at that he would be doing the friars a favor.

In vain did the monks insist upon the very modest social value of the prisoner. Misled by the letters of recommendation, Dali Mimmi refused to believe them. Five hundred escudos of gold, or no deal!

In desperation, Cervantes sought a solution which, although leaving him still prisoner, would help someone in the family and might offer a hope for him. He convinced his brother Rodrigo that he should be the one to be ransomed. Since the captors found no exultant letters of recommendation about Rodrigo, he was less important, hence cheaper on the slave market, and the funds entrusted to the friars would be sufficient for his release. Besides, Cervantes was hatching a plot that would result in his liberty. His brother would undertake the project from afar. His idea was to have Rodrigo procure a ship that would set sail at a determined date for a point along the Algerian coast where the prisoners would be waiting.

Rodrigo left with tears of sorrow and gratitude for his release, and Miguel began to prepare for his second attempt to escape. This time it would be more difficult in view of the logical distrust which his masters now harbored. Meanwhile, he gave vent to the anguish he felt at being abandoned in an *Epistle in Verse*, a petition which he sent to Mateo Vázquez, Secretary to the King and friend of the family:

> When I arrived, captive, and saw the land
> So renowned throughout the world, which in its bosom
> So many pirates harbors, welcomes, and keeps,
> There was no power to contain my weeping. . . .

The poet still breathed in the prisoner. The mentality of today no doubt finds it curious that a plea for help such as that sent to the royal government should be written in verse. Poetry, queen of the arts, was used then to convey praise as well as insults and for communications between lovers. Plays were completely in verse, and sometimes it was necessary to be a poet to enact administrative business or even to cry out from a dungeon for help.

Mateo Vázquez was occupied with a thousand problems of the court and so forgot the petition. Cervantes decided he would have to take things into his own hands if he ever expected to get out of that hell.

He began his operations. Needing a refuge, he found it in a secret cave in the garden of Hassan, the warden. Here fourteen conspirators assembled, escaping one at a time after freeing themselves of the shackles. Only at night, and then only one by one, did they dare to leave the cave for a breath of fresh air. Cervantes supplied them with their daily provisions, which he bought or was able to steal from his miserly captors. For seven long months he was aided in his task by a renegade, El Dorador (the gilder), who was to prove as willing to betray Allah as he had been to abandon the worship of the Virgin Mary.

In September, 1577, by the mysterious combined workings of a merchant, a liberated slave, and a new Christian prisoner, came the news that a Majorcan brig, chartered by Rodrigo, would on the following day come near shore across from the cave. Cervantes fled from his master's house that night and met with his companions. Now they had only to wait, embark, and escape.

The anguish in such a situation—the anxiety to escape, the fear of being captured, and especially the lack of confidence in the men who were helping them—was described years afterward in the *Quixote*, by Cervantes, reliving his own story. How well he understood men! The captives who had been freed so that they could return to liberate their companions did not do it "because once they had recovered their liberty, the fear of losing it again erased from their memory every obligation in the world." In his own case, it was a renegade whom he had to follow.

These were the contents of the second letter, and when we had all seen it, each one offered himself to be the ransomed man, and promised to go and to buy the vessel and to return with complete punctuality. I, too, offered to do the same. The renegade was opposed to all of this, saying that in no case would one man go out free before they all went together, because experience had taught him that those set free do not keep the promises they make in captivity. Important captives had often used that expedient to ransom someone who might go to Valencia or Majorca with money to outfit a ship and return for those who had ransomed him, but they never returned because once they had recovered their liberty, the fear of losing it again erased from their memory every obligation in the world.

Night after night they held their breath the better to hear the slightest sound that was to announce their liberty. Finally, they heard the muffled sound of approaching oars in the calm sea. The prisoners, flocking together, left the cave with the scant belongings they had packed for the escape. They could hear the oars coming closer and closer. Suddenly they heard shouts in Arabic and the patter of running feet. The rhythmic noise of the oars accelerated; now it was a strong and anguished beating like the hearts of those who were waiting. But as their hearts beat ever faster, the renegade disappeared into the night. On the enormous surface of the sea, there was no one.

"They did not dare to disembark," Miguel de Cervantes was to comment years later.

"They were surprised by a patrol of Moors and their only recourse was to flee," remarked another prisoner, perhaps more impartial.

Misfortune attracts misfortune. El Dorador, who up to this point had been helping them, now saw in the fiasco an occasion to betray them. He thought it would be simpler if they were denounced now, and he would be paid for his trouble. It would be a way to reconcile fear and lust for profit. He would hand them over.

Having been notified, the ruler of Algiers, Bey Hassán Bajá, ordered his soldiers to go to the cave. Demoralized, offering no resistance, the prisoners surrendered. One alone among them stepped forward to face the commander of the troops: "None of these Christians in here had anything to do with this affair, because I alone have been the instigator of everything and the one who has induced them to flee."

What Cervantes had done was very serious indeed. He was a Christian who had tried to escape and to help others escape, thus humiliating an Algerian and causing him to lose the profits of a possible ransom. According to the customs of the period, he should be put to death, and what is more, it could never be termed a merciful death. Impaling —that is, fixing the victim on a stake thrust through the body—hanging, or burning alive were customary punishments. This is what Miguel de Cervantes expected; in fact, it was what everyone who knew of the affair expected, being well aware of the Bey's cruelty.

However nothing of the sort occurred. The astonished captives commented on the strange benevolence that the Bey of Algiers showed toward Cervantes. He bought him from Dali Mimmi for five hundred escudos and locked him up in prison, naked and in chains, but alive. For what reason?

Let us consider a logical explanation of the Bey's behavior. He was evidently impressed by the courage of a man who declared himself the person solely responsible for a crime which obviously carried with it the death penalty. But he probably also saw in this gesture one more demonstration of what was being rumored in Algiers—that Cervantes was a person of high birth. The reason for such a deduction may seem strange today, but the people in those times were convinced that nobility of character was inseparable from nobility of blood, and that only aristocrats were capable of generous acts which were unknown to those of the lower classes.

When Ercilla, a writer contemporary with Cervantes, explains the discovery of America in the epic poem *Araucana*, he notes that Christopher Columbus believed himself to be of humble birth but states that this was not possible in view of his heroic deeds; therefore, he must have been of noble lineage, although unaware of it. This concept was so firmly rooted in the popular imagination that the Spanish word *villano*, meaning a man of a villa or country house, not an aristocrat, is related to the English word *villain*, meaning a man of unprincipled character. Only the noble, or as he was called in Spanish, *caballero*, was privileged to ride a horse (*caballo*); the villager went about on a donkey, the priest on a mule. Even today the notion exists that only the *caballero* is capable of generosity.

Hassán Bajá probably believed the same. It is one explanation for his not punishing an act of such dangerous rebellion. Apart from the moral impression which the prisoner created, it seems evident that Hassán was influenced in his decision by the idea that Cervantes was worth a profit, which he would lose by having him executed. Also, he must have thought that a man capable of such deeds should be in special custody immediately and with maximum security.

Thus Cervantes entered the most difficult phase of his prison life. When, in the *Quixote*, the "captive" speaks, it is the author proudly indulging in self-praise:

In Algiers I intended to seek other ways of accomplishing that which I so greatly desired, for I never gave up hope of obtaining my liberty. When my plans and efforts did not turn out as I intended, I did not despair but began once more to look for some new hope to sustain me, however feeble it might be. In this way I kept alive, shut up in a prison or house which the Turks call a *bagnio*, where they keep the Christian captives, those of the ruler as well as those of private individuals, and also those who are called the slaves of the *almacén*, that is to say, slaves of the municipality who are employed in public works and in other duties. With great difficulty did these last-mentioned recover their liberty, for they are held in common and have no particular master. There is no one with whom to bargain for their ransom, even though they might have the money. To these *bagnios*, as I have said, the private individuals of the town are in the habit of bringing their slaves, especially when they are about to be ransomed because there they can keep them unemployed and in security until their money arrives. The slaves of the Bey do not go out with the rest of the captives, unless their ransom is delayed, in which case, in order to make them write for it more insistently, they make them work and go for wood, which is no small labor.

Since it was known that I was a captain, I was among those to be ransomed. Although I told them of the impossibility of being redeemed because of my lack of means, nothing could keep them from adding my name to the list of gentlemen and those waiting to be ransomed. They put me in chains, more a sign that I was to be ransomed than a restraint. In this way I passed my life in that *bagnio* with other gentlemen and persons of quality selected and kept for ransom. Although hunger and nakedness troubled us at times, indeed almost always, nothing distressed so much as seeing and hearing at every turn, unequaled and unheard of cruelties that my master inflicted upon the Christians. Every day he would hang someone, impale another, cut the ears off yet another, and all this with so little provocation, or with none at all, that even the Turks knew that he did it for the pleasure of doing it, his nature being that of an assassin to the entire human race. The only one who got along with him was a Spanish soldier, a certain Saavedra, who, although he had done things which will remain in the memory of the people there for many years, and all of these things to recover his liberty, never received a blow nor was anyone ordered to strike him nor speak harshly to him. All of us feared he would be impaled for the least thing, and he, too, more than once expected it. If there were more time, I would tell you right here some of the exploits of that soldier which would entertain you and astonish you far more than my own adventures.

Meanwhile, in Madrid, the arrival of Rodrigo de Cervantes gladdened the hearts and motivated anew the conscience of the members of his family. Doña Andrea, the loose woman, and Doña Magdalena of the irreproachable conduct, experienced the same reaction when it was a question of saving their brother's life. In order to get together a sum of money, they sacrificed one of their most important hopes of ever marrying—their dowries. Without a dowry in the Spain of that time, a woman had little chance of matrimony.

But Cervantes could wait no longer, so he made two more attempts to escape by writing some letters to Oran and getting himself a boat. In the first, he had the aid of a faithful Moor, and in the second, that of a former Dominican friar, Blanco de Paz, who treacherously denounced him. The Bey, Hassán, threatened Cervantes with two thousand lashes, which was, in practice, a death sentence. A fraction of it would finish off the strongest man. One can sense the extraordinary and illogical influence that this wounded and crestfallen prisoner exercised over the powerful ruler, for Hassán did not carry out the sentence. Cervantes had to go on living.

But where was he going to live? Hassán had been dismissed from his position in Algiers and was preparing to return to Constantinople. Naturally he was taking with him his women, furnishings, jewels, and slaves. Just at the moment they were ready to embark, two Trinitarian monks arrived at the port of Algiers to see one of these prisoners —Miguel de Cervantes. They had brought the money that his family had so painfully collected, a quantity far short of five hundred escudos, the minimum amount which Hassán demanded for this captive. The bargaining went on, with no success, until the Bey decided to leave. Desperate, Father Juan Gil went seeking among the merchants of the port the two hundred and twenty escudos which they lacked. He obtained them and ran back to find that Hassán was already embarking. Among the slaves, herded together like sheep ready to be taken to Constantinople, was Cervantes. A finger pointed toward him and a voice was heard: "That one, let him go."

Amid the weeping of those who had to embark upon that almost certainly final journey Cervantes was ransomed. In the document of sale, he was described as "Resident of Madrid, medium build, well bearded, crippled in his left arm and hand, captive of the galley, *The Sun*, en route from Naples to Spain."

He had spent five years in prison. During that time he had collected stories, tales of events from those who had taken part in them, and had recorded experiences to which he had been a witness. Two plays, *The Bagnios of Algiers* and *The Traffic of Algiers*, were born of these memories, and so was the "Captive's Story," which is one of the best parts (for being the most deeply felt) of the *Quixote*. Nevertheless he had lost five years on his quest for glory and prosperity.

On the horizon Cervantes saw the Levantine coastline. Finally, in the port of Denia, he touched Spanish soil. By mid-December Cervantes was in Madrid.

He had left Spain's capital in 1568 to avoid a sentence which he considered harsh and unjust: "loss of his right hand and ten years of exile." Now, returning after twelve years, he had lost the use of his left hand and was battered in body and in soul.

Cervantes wept.

THE CIVIL SERVANT

In "The Watchful Guard," one of Cervantes' best *Interludes*, or short plays, there appears a soldier burdened with the tale of glory which he intends to use to obtain employment:

Master: Young man, what is it you want or expect, waiting here in front of this house?

Soldier: I want more than is good, and I am looking for more than I'll get. But who are you, sir, to ask me?

Master: I am the master of this house.

Soldier: You are Christina's master?

Master: That is right.

Soldier: Well then, sir, come near and have a look at this roll of papers. You will see that therein are the documents of my military service. Twenty-two certificates from twenty-two generals under whose banners I have served, not to mention thirty-four others by as many field marshals who have deigned to honor me.

Master: As far as I know, there have not been that many generals or field marshals in the Spanish Infantry in a hundred years.

Soldier: Sir, you are a peaceful man and have no reason to concern yourself with military matters. Take a look at these documents and you will see on them the names of all the generals and field marshals.

Master: I'll take your word for it. Why are you telling me all of this?

Soldier: So that you will see, sir, that these papers are proof of what I am about to tell you. I am being considered for the position of commandant in one of three fortified towns in the Kingdom of Naples: Gaeta, Barleta and Rijobes.

In a way, this is a caricature of the author, who after his past misfortunes felt that he should have compensation. Naturally he encountered difficulties, one of which was the then-current preoccupation of the Court. In 1580 all eyes were on Portugal, whose crown Philip II, King of Spain, was to seize. The great political problem of the day was the succession to the Portuguese crown. The Portuguese King, Don Sebastián, had died without a direct heir. There had been a period when the country was without a sovereign, owing to the attempt of the aged Cardinal Enrique, uncle of Don Sebastián, to obtain a dispensation from the Pope which would allow him to marry. He hoped thereby to produce an heir so that the monarchy would continue in the hands of the Portuguese. The Pope, a friend of Philip II, refused his request. The cardinal died shortly thereafter, and the Portuguese people realized it was going to be difficult to dispute the rights of the Castilian king, who, besides being Don Sebastián's closest relative, had on Portugal's frontier a strong army commanded by the Duke of Alba, the terror of Flanders.

As a matter of fact, the Duke of Alba marched onto Lusitanian soil and Philip was proclaimed King of Portugal. In addition to the Iberian Peninsula, Spain obtained the immense overseas territories which had been won by the soldiers and sailors of her neighbor nation. As the Pope had divided practically the entire world between the Spaniards and the Portuguese, Philip II was King not only of the American provinces which are today Chile, Peru, Colombia and Mexico, but also of Brazil. Not only did he possess the Philippines, but the Molucca Islands as well, which today comprise Indonesia and part of the coast of India. And if, through Spain, he occupied North Africa, as King of Portugal he now had the South, plus Mozambique and Angola. Truly the sun never set on his dominions.

Amid such wealth and power, why was there no position for one person who so very much merited it? Cervantes persisted in Madrid and even followed the court to Portugal. He continued to place his hopes in the secretary, Mateo Vázquez, the one to whom he had dedicated the verses but from whom he had received no reply. His ambition was to receive a military captaincy or a government appointment, although for the former he was at a disadvantage because of his useless left arm. For the latter he was probably qualified, but there were so many aspirants and so few positions.

Cervantes' record was excellent, but in that period there were many who could present equally good dossiers of their military service and years of captivity. What is more, his most brilliant feat was already becoming somewhat remote in time. Had he arrived shortly after the news of the great victory, possibly he might have obtained a prize, but nine years had passed since Lepanto. Now people were speaking of the victorious battle of Terceira (a Portuguese island in the Azores), where Alvaro de Bazán defeated the French who were attempting to aid the recalcitrant Prior of Crato, Portuguese pretender to the throne and last hope of the Portuguese who refused to accept the foreign king. As so frequently happened in his life, Cervantes arrived too late.

As time wore on and Cervantes spent the little money he had, his petitions became more modest in tone. If a permanent post was not possible, well then, perhaps some commission. They gave him one. He was to go to Oran in the service of the King to verify the possible existence of a Portuguese faction that favored the Prior of Crato and was opposed to the King's interest. It was a commission so secret that we scarcely know anything of it. He went, investigated, returned with his report, received one hundred ducats for travel expenses, was thanked for his services and dismissed.

In 1582 he was back in Madrid, frequenting its gossip centers and going to plays. Perhaps as a refuge, he felt like writing again. The result was *La Galatea*, a pastoral novel, a literary form which was very much in vogue. Upon selling it to an editor for 1,336 reales in 1584, Cervantes was at last able to pay his debt to Father Juan Gil, his liberator. He had unsuccessfully petitioned the state for this sum in December 1580, begging that witnesses be called to testify to his conduct in captivity and to the conditions of his ransom.

He makes an allusion to his first novel, completely conscious of its value, in the famous book-burning scene in the first part of *Don Quixote*:

". . . but what is that book lying next to it?"
"*La Galatea* by Miguel de Cervantes," answered the barber.
"That Cervantes has been a friend of mine for many years, and I know that he is more versed in misfortunes than in verses. His book contains some good ideas; it promises much and performs little. We shall have to wait for the second part which he has promised. Perhaps with corrections it will be accorded the favor which is now denied it. Meanwhile, keep it under lock and key in your lodging."

The following lines are from the first act of a play called

The Valencian Widow, by Lope de Vega. It was not to be the only time that this author would speak of Cervantes; it was one of the few times that he would speak well of him:

> This, then, is *La Galatea*,
> Which, if you desire a good book,
> You have but to ask for it.
> Its author was Miguel Cervantes,
> Who in Lepanto lost
> a hand. . . .

Lope de Vega was a playwright. What did the theater represent for a writer? Adulation by the public, fame, immediate success; in short, money. Spanish theater, as the world knows it, was in its beginnings during exactly this period in Cervantes' life. After the disappearance of Greek and Roman theater, drama was reborn in the bosom of the Church in miracle plays and other types of religious representations. The theater went on expanding its possibilities by using increasingly profane characters and expression until finally it was deemed better to remove it from the steps of the Church, where for years theatrical performances had been given.

The theater then went into the street. Lope de Rueda, a famous playwright of the period, took his plays on the road, stopping in different towns. He carried in his carts all the stage properties necessary to his company of actors.

Cervantes had a definite point of view about the theater, and he felt he had a specific role to play in it. He explained it himself: as Lope de Rueda had been an innovator, he— Cervantes—wished to renovate the stage. He says, in the Prologue to the *Interludes*:

There is one thing that you cannot deny, although it may

be immodest of me to say so: namely, that in my own plays, *The Traffic of Algiers*, *The Siege of Numancia* and *The Naval Battle*, which were produced in the Madrid theaters, I dared to reduce the plays from their conventional five acts to three acts. . . . I was the first to represent on stage the imagination and hidden thoughts of the soul, by presenting moral characterizations to the general and agreeable applause of the audience. I wrote, during that time, twenty to thirty plays, and all of them were produced with no cucumbers or things of the sort hurled on stage. The plays ran their course without hisses, catcalls or uproar. Then, occupied by other things, I abandoned my pen and the writing of plays, whereupon entered the monster of nature, the great Lope de Vega, who carried off the crown of drama. He made vassals of all the players, putting everyone under his jurisdiction. He filled the world with his own happy and well-constructed plays, and no matter how many of them he wrote (over ten thousand pages of them), all of them, and this is one of the great things one may say of them, have been produced, according to what one hears said of them. And as to the other playwrights, who are numerous, and who wanted to share the glory with him, their plays put all together would not equal half of what he has written.

In the 1580's theater was already installed in its permanent form in the court. Like many public amusements, it had been initiated with beneficent and charitable objectives. The *Confradías* (brotherhoods dedicated to pious works) built and administered hospitals in the capital. They were granted licenses to provide the places where plays could be presented because part of the proceeds of the performance would go to maintain their various hospitals. Until then, the theater had been frowned upon by many conservative persons.

They complained that being exposed to the supposed immorality of some love intrigues would open the eyes of the women who should dedicate themselves solely to sacred books. "What will women do reading about other people's love affairs in books which deal with nothing but the subject of love?" warned the intellectual, Juan Luis Vives, as early as 1523. The theater was attacked by the moralists as a pernicious element in the life of the people, and aside from the charitable objective just mentioned, it was maintained because several important gentlemen gave it their protection, thereby protecting its principal actors. "Never get involved with actors," Sancho Panza was to say later on in *Don Quixote*. "Remember they are merry folk of pleasure; everyone favors them and protects them, helps them and treats them with consideration, especially when they are members of the authorized royal companies, for nearly every one of them dresses and comports himself as a prince."

Those "merry folk of pleasure" put on their plays in a theater called a *corral*, an interior patio of a building. They rented the lower windows of the house (*aposentos*) to serve as a theater box or stall as it is known today, and the upper windows (*desvanes*) as the gallery. Beneath the *aposentos* was a semicircle of raised seats (*grada*), and in front of these, some benches and an open space of the patio where the *mosqueteros*, or boisterous crowd with less money, remained standing during the entire performance. Since their patience was limited and their reactions frequently disorderly, authors attempted to placate them with pleasing prologues to keep them from shouting or throwing vegetables on stage. Apart from the boxes where the elegant ladies discreetly sat, the audience was entirely male, with the exception of the *cazuela*, or "stew pan," at the rear of the *corral* in the part farthest from the stage. This was a gallery set apart for the women of the lower classes, who shouted back and forth with the men below. The men flattered them by throwing sweetmeats, water, and *aloja*, a fermented honey drink, at them. This "flirting" was what most irritated the moralists. The defenders of the theater reminded them that the proceeds from the sale of those refreshments also benefited the hospitals.

The performances were given in the daylight, and when the sun was strong, an awning was stretched over the heads of the spectators. The play began, announced by a trumpet blast, at two o'clock in the afternoon in the wintertime and at three o'clock in summer. The *loa*, or prologue, was recited, explaining what the play was all about. The stage sets were primitive, perhaps a painted tree or a cardboard wall. This explains why there is in the dramas of this period so much written description of the stage, which today, with all of the scenic effects and decorations available, seems redundant and rather boring.

Women did not appear on the stage until 1581; up to that time feminine roles were played by boys. The presence of women in the cast naturally increased the protection given by important persons. All Madrid gossiped about the reputations of the actresses, who were considered loose women, and people commented ironically on the patience of their husbands.

Cervantes was born with a love for the theater. As his alter ego, Don Quixote, says, "Since my childhood I have been crazy for the theater, and in my youth I was really stage struck." But apart from this, in the theater one could attain glory, fame, and fortune. The first of these satisfied the vanity of the author. The economic benefits, even if modest, were continuous because the plays were performed repeatedly. The writer sold the copyright of his play to the actor who was also the manager of the company, its impresario, and artistic director. The actor-manager of those days was a versatile figure who did everything.

Romance, too, came to Cervantes by way of the theater in the person of Ana Franca de Rojas, who was the prototype of the attractive, easygoing actresses of the day. It seems that there was nothing of emotional or artistic importance in this amorous episode of Cervantes'. No one has been able to encounter in his works the impassioned descriptions which writers usually dedicate to the memory of their great loves. Ana Franca brought nothing grandiose to the life of Cervantes, but she did bear him a daughter, Isabel, whom the author recognized by bestowing on her the name Isabel de Saavedra.

The proof of the small importance of the Ana Franca relationship in his life was that at the very time she was awaiting the birth of their child, Cervantes was planning to marry someone else. She was a girl living in Esquivias, in the province of Toledo, fairly well off, and only nineteen years old. Cervantes was then thirty-seven, and all the evidence indicates that it was a marriage arranged by friends who wished to see him settle down in a situation which, although mediocre, was at least secure, rather than struggle with the difficulties of the literary life. The family of the young lady immediately distrusted that impoverished gentleman from Madrid, no longer young, with even less glory than money, who arrogantly spoke of his military past, dazzling the simple country folk with his exploits, perhaps much like a conceited character in the *Quixote*:

About that time there came to our village one Vicente de la

55

Roca, son of a poor farmer of the region. He had returned from Italy and various other places, having been a soldier there. As a lad of twelve, he was carried off by a captain who happened to be passing through town with his company. Twelve years later he returned, dressed as a soldier, wearing all sorts of bright colors, covered with crystal trinkets and fine steel chains. One day he would put on one fancy outfit and the next day another, but all of them were flimsy, gaudy, of little weight and less worth. The country people, who by nature are malicious, are, when idle, malice itself. They took note, and counted one by one his costumes and fineries and discovered that he had three suits, of different colors, with stockings and garters to match. But he mixed and varied them to such an extent that if one did not count them, he would have sworn that he had more than ten suits of clothes and more than twenty plumes of feathers. Don't think that these details about the clothes are excessive because they constitute the main part of my story.

(In all of his works, Cervantes states precisely the value of being well dressed. One of the saddest scenes in the *Quixote* is the one in which the Knight has only green thread to repair a black stocking.)

He [de la Roca] used to sit on a bench under a large poplar tree in our market place, where he would keep us with our mouths gaping, listening to the exploits he used to tell us. There was no country in all of the world he had not visited, nor battle he had not fought in; he had killed more Moors than there were in Morocco and Tunis combined, and had engaged in more duels according to him than Gante and Luna, García de Paredes and a thousand others that he named; and in all of them he had come out the victor, without losing a single drop of blood. Then again he used to show us the scars of wounds, which although they were not visible, he would have us believe . . . resulted from musket shots received in various encounters and skirmishes. Finally, with unparalled arrogance, . . . he declared that his arm was his father, his deeds his ancestry, and that being a soldier, he owed nothing even to the king himself. In addition to these pretentions, he was something of a musician and could strum a guitar with such feeling that some said he could make its strings speak. He was also a poet, and for every trifling occasion in the town he would compose a poem a mile and a half long.

The young girl from the provinces fell in love with this man who had fought and suffered so much. She married him against the wishes of her family, who did not even attend the wedding, with the exception of one uncle, the priest who married them on the twelfth of December in 1584. (Among the relatives of the bride was a country squire, shriveled and thin, very vain of his lineage, whose name was Alonso Quijada; another was a priest who believed in the truth of the novels of chivalry. Both of them impressed Cervantes' imagination.)

Now Cervantes was married; *La Galatea* had been published. He had taken a decisive step in his personal as well as in his literary life. It seemed that he could look forward to what one would normally expect in such circumstances: a long succession of children and a long succession of publications.

But let us not forget that we are dealing with a man who tried to attain all heights and who did not completely achieve any one of them. Once more Destiny intervened in the life of the wounded hero of Lepanto. Cervantes did have a daughter, but she was not legitimate; she was not born of someone of whom he was proud, but rather of someone of whom he was ashamed, as was the other product of his blood, the long-ago, almost legendary, Promontorio. The correct and the normal seemed to be most difficult for Cervantes to obtain. His legal wife, Catalina, would never bear him a child. And in his production of literary offspring there was to be a tremendous interlude. He would wait twenty years after the appearance of *La Galatea* before the publication of his next book. Twenty long years!

Meanwhile, which direction should he take? Should he return to Esquivias to look after his wife's properties, settle down to a tranquil life, free from worries? Between 1585 and 1587 Cervantes vacillated between the urgencies of his soul. The literary life was closer to his heart, but it was not remunerative. The country life implied abandoning the court for the boredom of a small town, and the constant clashing with the ill will of Catalina's family, who continued to distrust him. The death of his own father, Rodrigo de Cervantes, a man as charming as he was unfortunate, only increased Miguel's restlessness.

As a recourse, he still had the theater. *The Siege of Numancia, The Traffic of Algiers*, which are still in existence, and *The Great Turquesca, The Naval Battle, Jerusalem, The Gallant Arsinda, The Treaty of Constantinople*, which have been lost, were produced during this period, and if not received with great enthusiasm, neither were "cucumbers or things of the sort hurled on stage," according to his own commentary. And so it appeared that the artistic and economic career of Miguel de Cervantes was to be in the theater.

This was not possible either. In the prologue to *Interludes*, those eight short comedies, Cervantes spoke of "the monster of nature, the great Lope de Vega, who carried off the crown of drama."

The statement is brief but categorical. Seldom has such brevity described a vital drama. Lope appeared in the life of Cervantes like a gigantic tree which was to cast its shadow over him forever. With a flutter of his cape, Lope displaced Cervantes in the theatrical world. Lope's works were soon the only ones produced, his name the only one mentioned with admiration in Madrid circles. We cannot underestimate the importance of the existence of this Madrilenian in the life of the gentleman from Alcalá. Cervantes' future was to a great extent dependent upon the literary displacement to which we refer. Lope de Vega's triumph in the field in which, for better or for worse, Miguel de Cervantes himself was evolving, was to send the latter into a government job, more days in prison, and finally, into writing *Don Quixote*.

If, from the historical perspective of today, we weigh the literary value of both authors, it is difficult for us to imagine that a Lope could have that much influence in destroying a Cervantes (although in the long run Lope contributed to Cervantes' deification). There are two reasons for it: one, the fashion of the day; the other, personality.

The fashion of the time, as we have said, was poetry. No one in this epoch following on the heels of the Renaissance could hope to succeed in the literary world unless he was capable of composing beautiful verses. On the stage a word in prose was never heard. For a writer to be well known, the indispensable qualification was to be a good poet. This obsession is implicit in *The Man of Glass*, who speaks for the writer himself. When someone asked of the hero if he were a poet, he answered, "I have not been so foolish as to have become a bad poet, nor so fortunate as to deserve to be a good one." A bit further on he said, "There were so few good poets, they were scarcely worth counting." That was the defense of a person who believed that he had never reached the point of being a good versifier, of one who, on another occasion, would say:

> I, who must ever strive, sleepless,
> To make it seem I am a poet,
> Which Heaven has denied me.

The only satisfaction to Cervantes' pride consisted in believing that the authentic, the good poets were minimal in number.

And the bad ones? Following his praise of the good ones with whom he wanted to include himself, but did not deserve to, he wrote a delightfully witty description of the bad poet who is convinced of his poetic genius: the one who in any gathering opportunely brings forth his latest composition and who, when no one is impressed with his reading, is quite astonished and blames his audience for not having paid more attention. He is a universal type who exists in all times and places. There is always one in any group. He may tell a joke or a story rather than recite poetry, but the main elements—his unjustified vanity, his petulance, his accusing his listeners of lack of understanding instead of recognizing his own deficiency—are the same today as always. Cervantes describes the type in *The Man of Glass*:

It is a sight to behold, one of those fledgling poets, when he wishes to recite a sonnet to those around him. How he makes excuses saying, "I beg your worships to listen to a little sonnet I composed last night on a certain occasion, which in my opinion is without value, but it has a little something, I don't know just what, of charm about it." And with this, he purses his lips, arches his eyebrows, ransacks his pocket, and among a thousand greasy, half-torn papers which contain a thousand other sonnets, he extracts the one he wishes to declaim, and finally recites it in a honeyed and affected tone. And if by chance, those who hear it, either from malice or from ignorance, fail to praise him, he says, "Either your worships have not understood the sonnet, or I have read it badly, so it will be well for me to recite it again, and I beseech your worships to pay more attention to it, because really the sonnet deserves it," and he begins all over again, with new gestures and new pauses.

In short, poetry was important, and to be a good poet was absolutely essential.

Lope de Vega was, without any doubt, a much better poet than Cervantes. The opinion of that time has not varied with subsequent literary criticism. Cervantes was, and is, a good poet. But Lope is one of the most sublime in the Spanish language.

There was, however, another reason for de Vega's ascendance, which in a society other than Spanish might not have had the same importance: the personality of these two rivals. All testimony agrees that Lope was outgoing, generous, and charming. From the beginning, life had treated him with greater generosity than it had Cervantes, and his appearance and character reflected it. He descended from a noble family from the province of Santander in the north of Spain. Although they were not wealthy, he had never seen the shadow of hunger at home, nor had he had to flee from city to city to evade prison because of debts or look for relatives to help pay them as did the family of Cervantes. Nor did he feel, as Cervantes did, the immense bitterness of having lost nearly five years of his life in an Algerian dungeon. In any comparison between the two writers, Lope nearly always has the advantage over Cervantes as far as luck is concerned. Even in his love affairs, Lope was more brilliant. In the theatrical world he had relationships with Marta de Nevares and other important actresses who could help him get his plays produced, while Cervantes involved himself with the insignificant Ana Franca de Rojas. Following the custom of the times, both humiliated themselves by asking noblemen who had more ancestry than talent to deign to sponsor them, that is to say, pay them for their literary efforts. But Cervantes dedicated *La Galatea* to the Duke of Béjar, who ignored him, and only many years later did he receive financial help from the generous Count of Lemos. From the very beginning, Lope approached the Duke of Sessa, who handsomely rewarded him with money and with legal protection in return for the dedications of Lope's works to him, and for the letters the author wrote, entertaining his benefactor with the most sordid adventures and the latest gossip of the court.

The human character is composed of virtues and defects, some inherent and some created by life's experience. Cervantes' pessimism was probably born with him, and adversity helped to aggravate it. The natural optimism of Lope was strengthened by his social and literary successes. He became so firmly established that not even his participation in the worst disaster of the epoch, which marked the beginning of Spain's decline, was sufficient to destroy his faith in his country or in his own destiny. Lope de Vega, who took part in the defeat of the Great Spanish Armada, sang continuously in his works of the positive aspects of the Spaniard: his bravery, his strong religious faith, his patriotism. Cervantes, who had an important role in the most glorious Spanish victory of the period, the battle of Lepanto, poured into his fundamental work, the *Quixote*, sadness and bitterness.

The Spaniard has always given great importance to a man's physical appearance, and so it is entirely possible that, apart from his literary gifts, Lope owed some of his success to his smile. The arrival of Cervantes at the house of an actor-manager, his play under his arm, must have been accompanied by a resigned sadness of anticipated defeat, of one who already knew that the answer would be "no," and so resented beforehand the negative reply because he was aware of the value of his work. Shabbily dressed, his left arm paralyzed, awkward in speech, according to his own confession practically a stammerer, and perhaps, as has been said, guilty of bad breath, Cervantes was no competitor of that dapper gentleman, who, even after changing his courtly clothes for those of a priest, emanated elegance and finesse. Other conditions being equal, actors would always take Lope's play. But conditions were nearly always unequal—in favor of the latter.

In the 1580's the paths of the two great writers crossed for the first time, and would continue to do so for the rest of Cervantes' life. The life of one was to influence that of the other even when their orbits seemed most distant from each other. For example, as we have said, Lope de Vega took part in the Invincible Armada. Cervantes did not, but that same naval expedition indirectly launched him into one of the saddest periods of his life.

The Armada, the Great Armada that Philip II was preparing against England, gave Cervantes the government post that he had been seeking in vain for so many years. Now in view of the difficulty that he was having to establish himself in the theater, he needed it more than ever.

Early in 1587 he left for Seville, having been appointed a "commissary." His function was to requisition food supplies, mainly wheat and olive oil, in the region of Andalusia to supply the needs of the fleet for the impending expedition against England, which was to end once and for all the period of Elizabeth of England—the double enemy of Spain: English and Protestant. A children's song of the time reflects this well:

> My brother Bartolo
> is going off to England.
> He will seize Francis Drake
> and then kill the Queen.
> He is going to bring me
> as a gift from the war,
> a Lutheran fellow
> bound up in chains,
> and a Lutheran lady,
> Señora grandmother.

The war against England was a tremendously popular undertaking because for the Spaniards of the epoch it combined two important objectives: It would put an end to the English pirate ships that were attacking Spanish vessels, returning to Spain with gold and silver from America, and it would terminate the bulwark of heretics which the British Isles represented. Little did it matter that the religion was Anglican and not Lutheran. The Spaniard of the time did not find it necessary to be too precise in order to abominate a religion counter to his own, which was "the only true religion."

But this gigantic undertaking—going off to destroy the enemy on his own soil—needed gigantic organization: recruiting men, arming ships, providing them with sufficient supplies for a long military operation. Cervantes was just one more among the commissaries who went from town to town to encourage, convince, and, if necessary, to intimidate the citizens until they handed over their share of wheat and olive oil needed for His Majesty's Service. It was disagreeable work. In the first place, in a poor region where the harvests were uncertain due to the primitive methods of cultivation, the quotas fixed by the commissaries were frequently several times higher than the actual harvests. In the second place, the farmers were paid a ceiling price which was much lower than the one they could get by selling in the free market, which compensated them for losses suffered during bad years when the harvest was scanty or nonexistent. Also, the fixed price was supposed to be paid upon delivery, but in practice the State paid only after great delays. The royal treasury was always short of funds, in spite of the immense treasures of gold arriving from the Spanish possessions in America. So in spite of the patriotic sentiments of the people and their awareness of the necessity of defeating the enemy in a definitive battle, the task presented endless problems for the supplier of the Royal Provisions.

It has been traditional in Spain, and still is, for the people to distrust the bureaucracy and the functionary or civil servant. Even when a king was at the height of his prestige, the citizens distrusted the person who presented himself in His Majesty's name and in his name collected. They feared, and often rightly so, that the commissary was thinking more of his own needs than of those of His Majesty. A long series of cases of corruption involving certain noblemen in highest government positions had given a bad reputation to the kind of functionary that Cervantes had now become.

It was not exactly a suitable type of work for a poet, a dramatic author, a bucolic novelist. Nevertheless Cervantes accepted it because it paid reasonably well, when and if he received his salary (twelve reales a day, which roughly equaled the price of three acres of wheat), and it gave him a certain authority which flattered his frequently wounded pride. He had the right to enter everywhere, use force, pay the established price, provided that the royal treasury had, in its turn, sent the money.

He was soon beset with problems. Ecija, the hottest city in Andalusia, which merited the title "the frying pan of Andalusia," refused to give its requirement of wheat because it still had not been paid for that requisitioned the previous year. But Cervantes had definite orders: Break down doors, search the premises, seize the hidden commodities, arrest the recalcitrants. He had the authorization of the King and was to stop at nothing. The townspeople were unable to offer legal opposition, but there were those who made use of their ecclesiastical status. The vicar of Ecija accused Cervantes of seizing the Church's property, which was exempt from requisition, and therefore excommunicated him. In reality, considering the innumerable properties of the Church at that time, such an exemption was impossible. But the Cathedral Chapter of Seville, which did not dare excommunicate the King who was responsible for the order, avenged themselves on the poor commissary who did no more than carry it out. Such a punishment was no small thing. During a time when being a good Catholic was practically synonymous with being a good Spaniard, it was extremely grave to be barred from entering a church and receiving the blessed sacrament. A person who had been excommunicated was pointed to on the street, the neighbor's children no longer associated with his, he was considered almost a pestilent.

Cervantes went humbly from one ecclesiastical authority to another, explaining what had happened, until he succeeded in getting them to annul his excommunication sentence. He could breathe easily once more, for he was again officially a good Catholic—until the following year. This time it was a sacristan of Castro del Rio who resisted when Cervantes confiscated his quota of wheat. Cervantes had him jailed, and again the Church angrily rose up in defense of one of her humble servants. Again Cervantes was excommunicated, this time by the vicar general of Córdoba. Cervantes' name was exposed to public disgrace by exhibiting it on the bulletin board outside the church door, as it had been shortly before in Seville. He had passed through these two cities as a child and adolescent, and now they were seeing his name slandered in this infamous manner. In vain did Cervantes bring out his orders, which stated word for word: "To confiscate by force whatever quantity of wheat and barley that was to be found in the possession of whomever, whether his status be ecclesiastical or secular. . . ." Perhaps as one commentator has suggested, the problem was that the sacristan was not yet a priest, but he had already left his secular condition, and in this particular case there were no precise instructions. Once more Cervantes finally obtained absolution after another thousand visits and explanations.

He had more problems in Ecija, where he lacked money to pay for the wheat he collected. Ecija petitioned the King to get rid of Cervantes, "who was taking the bread out of their mouths." The people of Marchena made the same request. They started saying that he was collecting more wheat and barley than had been indicated. There were rumors about the way he kept his accounts.

Could this possibly be true? In the lives of great men there always exists some difficult and touchy point. Biographers have a tendency to become enamored of their subjects. It is a reaction that comes from the initial admiration they feel, which then becomes exaggerated as the hours accumulate in the study of their hero. Often the biographer refuses to admit that the subject to whom he had dedicated so much time and effort might be capable of anything that would spoil his total perfection. The writer must be generous and noble, incapable of suggesting the slightest stain upon the personality of his hero. Thus is born a cult which is difficult to combat, because those who proclaim it are the ones with the most erudition and are most qualified on the subject.

As to the case at hand, that of Cervantes' possible administrative corruption as Commissary for His Majesty in Andalusia, one must ask to what extent the accusations defaming him were an attempt on the part of the townspeople to rid themselves of a commissary who was tireless in his demands for quantities of wheat and oil which they did not want to contribute, and to what extent they were true.

Cervantes' biographers become indignant at the mere mention of the possibility that the gentleman from Alcalá might have been capable of diverting a single cent from the Royal Treasury, or of accepting a little bribe to forget this or that rich citizen when his required amount of wheat was due. Astrana Marín, the most conscientious of the

Cervantine scholars, points out, on the other hand, that in Ecija, Cervantes did make a mistake in his calculation, to his own loss. It is a weak defense. A good administrator should never make a mistake against himself because this indicates that on some other occasion he might make one in his favor, intentionally or not.

Documents are studied with the mind, but they are interpreted by the heart of the examiner, especially when they concern a case which infatuates as does that of Cervantes. Things become not what they are but what "they should be." Astrana Marín himself scrupulously admits that Cervantes promptly appeared in Seville with plenty of money, which he spent on diverse purchases and gifts. Knowing that Cervantes' income was meager, and always late, how does one explain such opulence at the very moment that he was administering funds which did not belong to him? Astrana Marín looks for an explanation which might satisfy both his conscience as a historian and his desire to absolve Cervantes of all suspicion of appropriating public funds. He says that that money most surely came from gambling. Cervantes was as much addicted to card playing as were all of the men of time. Many quotations from his works give proof of his knowledge of cards. But Astrana's deduction is excessively generous, considering his name and reputation as a scholar.

What did Cervantes really do in his position as Commissary of the King? There are various possibilities for the impartial biographer. The accusations could have been, in truth, slander, and his unexpected wealth a product of good luck at cards. He could have made the mistake because of a lack of administrative ability inherited from his father and aggravated by his own impracticality. Or could he simply have felt that the money, though not legally his, morally belonged to him? It was the minimum pay for various services to the King for which he had never been remunerated; it was the minimum compensation for his sufferings in the prison of Algiers, or perhaps a reparation for his bad luck in the theater.

It was possible, and if so, there is no reason to be overly scandalized because of it. His greatness as a writer does not waver from its sublimity in spite of that possible human weakness. The picaresque life of Villon in no way dimmed his poetry, nor did the homosexuality of Oscar Wilde spoil his plays.[3]

Guilty of embezzlement or not, Cervantes felt free to ask for a better position in the Indies. ("The Indies" meant, at that time, the Spanish possessions in America.) They were a natural refuge for the Spaniard who had failed in his native land. As a character in the short novel *The Jealous Extremaduran* says:

Not many years ago a gentleman of noble parentage set out from Extremadura, as did another Prodigal, and wandered through various parts of Spain, Italy and Flanders, squandering his years as well as his fortune. After many travels (by now his parents were dead, and his inheritance spent), he happened to stop in the great city of Seville, where he found it only too easy to finish spending the little money he had left. So seeing himself so short of funds, and with few friends, he resorted to the same remedy to which so many others ruined in that city have recourse: that is, a voyage to the Indies, the refuge and shelter of the desperadoes of Spain, the sanctuary of the bankrupt, safe-conduct of murderers, shelter and cover of gamblers, called sharpers by some, the lure of loose women, the common deception of many and specific relief of few. In short, he had arrived at a time when a fleet was preparing to leave for America. He came to an understanding with the admiral, and furnishing himself with provisions and other necessaries, he embarked at Cádiz, and said farewell to Spain. The fleet weighed anchor, and amid general rejoicing, it set sail in the favorable winds and in a few hours they had lost sight of land and found themselves in the vast expanse of the great ocean.

Cervantes wrote the following petition in the year 1590, hoping to obtain the much-desired post in the New World:

Your Majesty:

Miguel de Cervantes declares that he has served Your Majesty for many years in campaigns at sea and on land such as came his way in the last twenty-two years. In particular, he took part in the great battle of Lepanto, where he sustained various wounds, including an injury from an arquebus which resulted in the loss of a hand; in the following year he served at Navarino and later in Tunis and La Goleta. Traveling to the capital, with letters from Don Juan of Austria and the Duke of Sessa, which recommended him to Your Majesty, he was taken prisoner on the galley *The Sun*, along with his brother who has also served Your Majesty during the same campaigns. Both were taken to Algiers, where to raise money for their ransom they exhausted all of their property as well as that of their parents and the dowries of two unmarried sisters who were reduced to poverty in order to ransom their brothers. After their liberation they served Your Majesty in Portugal and in the Azores under the Marquis of Santa Cruz, and at the present time they are still serving Your Majesty, one of them as an ensign in Flanders; while the other, Miguel de Cervantes carried letters and instructions to the Alcalde of Mostagan, carried out Your Majesty's order in Oran, and since then has been employed by the Navy in Seville in matters concerned with the Armada, under Antonio de Guevara. The above is confirmed by documents. In all of this time Miguel de Cervantes has been granted no favor. Now he humbly begs and requests to be given, if

Your Majesty sees fit to bestow it upon him, any one of the three or four positions presently vacant in the Indies, namely that of the auditor's office in the New Kingdom of Granada; the governorship of the province of Soconusco in Guatemala; or the accountancy for the galleys of Cartagena, or magistrate of the city of La Paz. Any one of these offices which Your Majesty would confer upon him, he will accept, being a man of skill and sufficient worth to merit the favor of Your Majesty, because his desire is to continue always in the service of Your Majesty and thus end his life, as his forefathers had done, which would be a great favor and mercy for him.

In this petition Cervantes exaggerated somewhat. He had lost the use or movement of his hand, but it remained in place. Also he used deliberately vague terms so that it seemed, upon reading, that both brothers fought in the Azores, when it was really only his brother Rodrigo who was in that campaign.

The Indies positions wavered between what we today would call those of military intendancy or those which were purely civil-service jobs. A man of Cervantes' position should have easily obtained them without too many connections. But the reply scribbled in the margin of his request, as was the custom, was negative, stating, "Let him find something here in Spain, which may be granted to him."

Scholars of Cervantes' life have given free rein to their imaginations regarding this attempt which failed. Almost all are sure that it was most unfortunate, and then, after attacking the decision that so badly rewarded the virtues of the hero, they congratulate themselves that it turned out this way, because, they affirm, had Cervantes gone off to America for the rest of his life to fill one of these positions, he might never have written the *Quixote*.

It seems most likely that the *Quixote* would have been born exactly the same, for the author was already carrying it inside of him. He had already met the proud country squire named Quijada and the cleric who believed in the novels of knight-errantry, and the immortal literary personage was developing within him as does a child in its mother's womb. What hunger led him to create, could perhaps have resulted from the leisure of an easy life. The *Quixote* had to be born. But had the work been written without economic pressures upon its author, it might not have had the formal defects which appear especially in the first part of a book written in haste and extended without measure, in which contradictions and forgetfulness abound.

Meanwhile, as if to frustrate more completely his labors as commissary, the Armada, about which he had been so concerned, had returned defeated by storms and the more modern vessels of the English. It had been a confrontation of two epochs of navigation. The Spanish galleys, as in Lepanto, carried huge infantry forces to assault the enemy vessel and fight hand to hand. The English had understood that it would not be necessary to grapple and board the adversary's ships in an open battle in order to win. It would be sufficient to employ their superior artillery and destroy with cannons those huge floating fortresses. The English then escaped contact by fleeing in their lighter, faster ships.

The disaster of the Armada surprised Europe and stupefied the Spaniards. Accustomed to seeing the hand of God in everything, they were unable to understand how He had conceded the victory to the enemies of the true religion, that is, to the Protestant English. Some theologians said that the reason must be found elsewhere. Father Rivadeneyra, who had exhorted the soldiers to join the liberating crusade to England, now maintained that evidently the cause of the defeat was that the expeditionaries had not been motivated solely by the love of their religion and the defense of their country; they had been goaded as well by obscure feelings of revenge and desire for spoils. This human impurity was what caused the failure of the divine undertaking. But the fact that there had been a storm, that the English navigators, accustomed to the waters of the Channel, had the better of them, only made the Spanish, with their Mediterranean point of view, all the more convinced that defeat was not a case of British military superiority but rather a decision from Heaven.

Cervantes echoed the same general idea when he left his administrative duties for a moment to raise his voice once again as a poet, beseeching Mother Spain not to see it as a disgrace that her sons returned after having "filled the ocean with their misfortunes." It was not the skill of the enemy that turned them back, he averred, but the relentless sea elements that had consented that "the enemy raise his head a little."

This was the last "positive" poetry that Cervantes wrote about the society around him. The parallel between his own misfortunes and those of his country, now on the road to decline, caused his poetry to change from verses full of faith to those of irony and bitterness. What most irritated Cervantes was the bombastic style of the men of his day, who had conserved nothing more than the appearance of the former heroes. This anomaly was manifest in the Earl of Essex's attack on Cádiz eight years after the

Invincible Armada. While the Englishman was sacking the city, the Spanish were making ostentatious preparations for combat under the command of one Captain Becerro, who was planning its liberation. By the time the Spanish militia marched into Cádiz to avenge themselves, the English had left the town in ruins and were on the high seas. How far we are from the sonnet to Isabella Valois and to the heroes of the African coast in the stinging sonnet that Cervantes wrote to satirize these men, even using their own names. He compares the militia to the images carried by religious brotherhoods in the procession during Holy Week, saying that they frightened the mob but not the English. He mocked their Pigmies and Goliaths, alluded to Captain Becerro, whose name in Spanish means "calf": ". . . the calf bellowed and put his squad in file; the sky grew dark, and the ground was seized with rumbling, threatening total ruin," and he ends the poem with reference to "their triumphal march into Cádiz, well after the enemy had fled, leaving it safe for the Great Duke of Medina."

Cervantes' fortunes in Andalusia went from bad to worse. New superiors demanded that he explain the management of his accounts, and on one occasion his replies did not satisfy them, and he was imprisoned. It was the greatest bitterness of his life. This time he was not arrested by the enemies of his religion and his country as he had been in Algiers. He was locked up by his own people. It happened precisely when he had intended to return to the theater and had signed a contract with the actor-manager Rodrigo Osorio, who had commissioned him to write six plays at fifty ducats each. With the self-assurance that was always a part of him, in spite of the misfortunes which plagued him, Cervantes added a rather arrogant clause: Rodrigo Osorio would not have to pay him for each play if after the performance of it, "it should appear that it is not one of the best in Spain. "

It was the pride of a man too sure of himself, making a promise he could not fulfill. He was released from prison on bail, but his problems pursued him. Some years later, having to send a large amount of money to Madrid and considering the transportation of the times (a long journey on horseback), it occurred to him to deposit the sum of 7,400 reales with a Sevillian merchant in exchange for a receipt and letter of credit to present at his branch office in Madrid. When he arrived in the capital, he could not collect the money because it no longer existed. The merchant had declared bankruptcy. His Majesty's government, in this case with reason, considered Cervantes responsible, and he was again imprisoned, this time for three months. Although there are those who see all of those incidents as a conspiracy against Cervantes, it is easier to believe that at best our writer was in no way a practical man. As to the discrepancies in his accounts, possibly Cervantes added to his traveling expenses the salary that was coming to him and which he saw no other way to collect, an arrangement that the government would not accept because it wanted to collect what money was owed the State, and in turn, pay the debts it had incurred, in a precise way, one at a time.

His possible theatrical career, which seemed about to have a new beginning, ran into another difficulty, still more serious than that of imprisonment. Philip II had closed the theaters of the capital in May, 1598, in accordance with advice of the theologians who, chafing a bit over the defeat of the Armada, passed the following judgment: "People are drawn to idleness, delights and pleasures, and their minds are turned from warlike pursuits; and with the indecent dances that these comedians everyday invent, and with the festivals, banquets, and comedies, the people of Spain are becoming soft and effeminate and unfit for work and war."

Also these were years of mourning for Cervantes. He had lost his mother, Leonor de Cortinas, that energetic woman who had done so much to secure his ransom, and Ana Franca de Rojas, mother of his daughter Isabel. The latter had been placed with his sister Magdalena to help her in the house and, in return, receive an education.

His legitimate wife was still in Esquivias. Despite the persistence of biographers in extolling the virtues of Cervantes, they never manage to endow him with any love for Doña Catalina. His sojourns in the village became increasingly less frequent, scarcely a few days now and then to sign a will or other business papers. Then he would leave to return to work in Andalusia or to amuse himself in Madrid.

Philip II died on September 13, 1598. In spite of having served him brilliantly, Cervantes had received nothing but rebuffs from him, and he dedicated no verses of eulogy to His Majesty. On the contrary, he took advantage of the presence of a sumptuous and exaggerated tumulus—the symbolic funeral mound erected in the cathedral of Seville for the last rites of the King—to satirize the type of braggart, so typical of Spanish society, who was to appear several times in his work. In this disrespectful sonnet he caustically criticizes the vain ostentation displayed in the final honors to his king and compares Seville to a second

Rome. The following is an admirable translation by the English poet James Y. Gibson. It is Cervantes himself who, upon entering the cathedral, gives his reaction at viewing the tumulus:

> I vow to God such grandeur stuns my brain!
> I'd give a crown its wonders to detail;
> For such a grand machine on such a scale
> Beggars description, makes invention vain.
> Now, by the living Christ, each piece, 'tis plain,
> Is worth a million! Pity it should fail
> To last an age! Hail grand Sevilla, hail,
> In wit and wealth a second Rome again!
> I'd wager that the soul of the deceased,
> On such a sight as this to gloat and gaze,
> Hath left its joys eternal in the skies.
> A listening puppy answered: "I at least,
> Sir soldier, doubt not what your honor says,
> Who dares to think the opposite he lies!"
> On this, to my surprise,
> The stripling stinted, fumbled with his blade,
> Looked sideways, vanished, and no more was said.

THE WRITER

Philip III was now king. He was brilliant, pompous, pleasure-loving, and addicted to both religious and social festivities. The court began to spruce up again. The favorite, the Duke of Lerma, openhandedly squandered money which he later recovered by selling government positions. The austerity of the custom of wearing black clothes, which symbolized the gloominess of Philip II, gave way to elegant and colored raiment.

The gossips rumored that the merchants of Valladolid had paid the Duke of Lerma for arranging to have the entire capital transferred to that city, abandoning Madrid. (A few years later he would accept a similar offer from the former capital to move it back to Madrid.)

Naturally, the theaters again opened their doors. It would have been a fine opportunity for Cervantes to launch the comedies that he had projected in his mind, but as so frequently in his life, he arrived too late. The Spanish theater of the epoch was completely in the hands of the great Lope de Vega, who was lauded for everything—his poetic grace, and as we have said, even for his physical appearance as he walked through the streets of Madrid, greeting his friends and acquaintances. He was a man of intense personality, who was as violently attracted to carnal appetites as he was to mysticism. The former made him the friend of actresses of every kind, and the second impelled him to become a priest, which proved insufficient to restrain him from his former habits. As a symbol of his previous behavior, he even retained his worldly mustache, which irritated the bishop, who made him shave it off. His amorous adventures did not cease with his religious vows. However there was no hypocrisy whatever in Lope. Having sinned, he lamented, wailed, and prayed with the same violence that characterized his transgression. His sonnets of remorse after the fall are among the most beautiful in the Castilian language. He was as sincere in sinning as he was in repenting.

"As good as Lope," the people in the street used to say. His life was already a gigantic myth and his facility for literary production was the talk of the town. In one of his plays he says that his verses "passed from the muses to the theater in twenty-four hours." On another occasion he establishes the number of plays he has written at fifteen hundred. The figure is probably exaggerated because it would have necessitated a practically impossible amount of work divided into his days of production. Besides, only some four hundred and seventy of his dramatic works have come down to us. In the case of an author so admired and so frequently quoted as was Lope, it is difficult to believe that so many others could have been lost. But even this number indicates an immensely rich literary production. Indeed the rapidity with which he wrote probably impaired the quality of his work.

In his plays he celebrated those qualities the Spanish loved in themselves: patriotism, religion, love for their king. The most humble of the audience felt satisfaction when he learned from Lope's verses that honor did not consist in being the son of a duke, but was rather a concept of the soul, and that from the most noble to the most plebeian, everyone could and should kill whoever might offend him. Such was the aureole of grandeur that Lope radiated among the people.

This grandeur naturally provoked enemies among his colleagues, some of whom questioned his position in the literary republic. The Golden Age, which refers to a period in letters roughly between 1560 and 1660, produced in this brief space too many good writers to peaceably share the fame. Their rivalry was reflected, according to the fashion of the day, in innumerable satires in verse which respected neither the privacy nor the physical defects of their targets. Lope, occupying the loftiest place, was the object of many literary attacks because of his haughtiness. For example, in *La Filomena*, Lope described the Castalian Springs[4] "where drank Homer, Virgil and another whom I shall not name." (In a copy of the book now in the National Library of Madrid, there is an indignant marginal note from the pen of Góngora, the greatest Spanish poet of the late Golden Age, saying, "If you mean yourself, Lope old boy, you are an idiot with neither art nor judgment.")

In the face of these assaults, Lope naturally reacted with the indignation of one who, from such Olympian heights, finds it impossible to believe that anyone should want to attack him. Satiric verse was answered with satiric verse, malicious phrases with malicious phrases.

Cervantes was among Lope's enemies because the latter had cut short the dramatic career in which Cervantes had planned to find glory and fortune. Feeling himself to be as great as his rival, Cervantes could not understand or tolerate the fact that life had treated them so differently. But he manifested his antagonism in a different way from that of the other writers. While Góngora, Ruiz de Alarcón, and later Quevedo openly insulted Lope and were violently answered by him, Cervantes played his cards in a more subtle but perhaps more vindicative manner. He clearly registered his bitterness in the prologue of a book which he was patiently writing during those years after he resigned from his job as commissary. It started out as a short novel which kept expanding as it developed. The original idea for it had come to him a long time ago, as we have already seen. Two of his wife's relatives, a poor but proud country squire and the priest who believed in the books of chivalry, had merged into one figure known as the authentic Don Quixote, born "In a village of La Mancha, whose name I do not wish to recall. . . ."

The book was born in the jail of Seville, "where every discomfort has its lodging and every sound its abode," a book in which the author combined his military experience of Lepanto with his administrative position in Andalusia; his student days of Alcalá with those of his imprisonment in Algiers.

The numerous misfortunes of his eventful life furnished him with an unlimited series of human types to whom he could refer: the galley slave, the innkeeper, the soldier, the actor, the fencing master, the shepherd, the duke. All of the innumerable characters who appear in the *Quixote* were old acquaintances of Cervantes, and he viewed them from the privileged position of his alter ego, Don Quixote, who was almost the same age as he, and, like his creator, had dreamed, and had lost. And with him his country had gone from Lepanto to the disaster of the Armada. From the chivalric ideal to the courtly dance, *Don Quixote* is the history of Cervantes and of Spain.

The most brilliant work of peninsular literature is held together with a bitterness which is alleviated, or made more acrid, only by its humor, which is sometimes gentle and resigned and sometimes sarcastic.

The *Don Quixote* was for Cervantes, now approaching sixty, an attempt at catharsis, at freeing himself of all he carried within him by telling it to a world that had treated him so badly. His first thrusts appear in the prologue, against that lordling, that overly conceited author who was attempting to gobble up the entire literary pie without leaving a crumb to fellow writers in the republic of letters. But he made that attack without naming the hated rival. Góngora, a great and admired poet, although at times not understood, could permit himself the luxury of insulting Lope by name. Cervantes, on the other hand, demonstrating his tremendous inferiority complex before the colossus who surpassed him in elegance, distinction, fame, and wealth, fired his attacks without mentioning Lope directly. He merely points out ironically in the prologue that he is not going to introduce his book with a string of maxims of the classical writers such as Aristotle, Plato, or of the doctors of the Holy Church. He goes on to say that he will not include unnecessary sonnets by aristocratic Spaniards who might praise his book, nor will he boast of his heraldry and coat of arms; that is to say, he will have none of that which Lope de Vega customarily included in his books. As Cervantes says in the Prologue to *Don Quixote:*

I should like to bring you the story pure and naked, unadorned by a prologue, and the endless string of sonnets, epigrams and eulogies which are customary at the beginning of books. I admit that although it cost me some work to compose the story itself, I found no greater task than writing this preface which you are reading. Many times I picked up my pen to write it, and many times I laid it down, not knowing what to write. Once, in such a moment of suspense, with the paper in front of me, my pen over my ear, my elbow on the desk and my hand on my cheek, thinking of what I would say, there entered unexpectedly a witty and intelligent friend of mine, who seeing me so pensive, inquired as to the reason. Not wishing to conceal it from him, I told him I was thinking about the prologue I had to write for the story of Don Quixote, and it was giving me so much trouble that I was disposed not to write one, nor even to publish the exploits of such a noble knight. I asked him how he expected me not to be concerned about what that venerable lawmaker, called the public, will say when they see me, after so many years of sleeping in the silence of oblivion, now come forth with all my years on my back with a story dry as a rush, lacking in invention, wanting in style, poor in conceits, and devoid of all erudition and doctrine, without quotations in the margins nor notes at the end of the book, when I see that other books, whether they be fabulous or profane, are full of quotations from Aristotle, Plato and the whole band of philosophers so as to dazzle their readers and lead them to look upon the author as eloquent and scholarly. And when they quote from the Holy Scripture one would think they are so many Saint Thomases and other doctors of the Church. They are so clever in maintaining a solemn presence that in one line they have described a distracted lover and in the next a Christian sermon that is a delight to hear and read. All of this will be absent in my book for I have nothing to quote in the margin, nor notes to add at the end, nor do I know to which authors I should give credit by listing them all alphabetically as they all do beginning with Aristotle and ending with Xenophon, Xoilus or Zeuxis, although one was a slanderer and the other a painter. My book will also be lacking in sonnets at the beginning, sonnets at least whose authors are dukes, marquises, counts, bishops, great ladies or celebrated poets; although if I were to ask two or three colleagues of mine, I know they would furnish me with them, and of such excellence that they could not be equaled by the most renowned poets in our country. In short, my dear friend, I went on, I am determined that *Don Quixote* shall remain buried in the archives of La Mancha until Heaven provides someone to adorn him with the things he lacks, for I find myself unable to remedy the situation because of my insufficiency of learning, and because I am by nature too lazy to go looking for authors to say for me what I can say without them. This is the cause for the bewilderment and daydreaming in which you found me; that is reason enough to put me in this state you have just heard.

His friend, in the prologue, replied, saying that the easiest thing of all to remedy is the lack of sonnets, epigrams, and eulogies written by important titled people in the beginning of his book. He tells the author to write them himself and afterward baptize them with any name he fancies. And as to the want of marginal quotations, all he needs to do is to drag in some trite Latin phrases which either he knows by heart or can easily look up. If necessary he can quote the Holy Scriptures in Latin, and with these scraps of Latin and others of the sort he might cause himself to be taken for a grammarian, which is honorable and profitable these days. The problem of the bibliography can be easily resolved by looking up some book which has them all from A to Z and copy the entire list as it stands. It does not matter that he will have little need to refer to them, and perhaps some may be so foolish as to believe he has drawn from all of them for his simple tale. If nothing else, such a bibliography will give his book an unexpected authority, for no one will take the trouble to find out if he has used all these authors or not, for he has nothing to gain by it. Then his friend concludes that since Cervantes' purpose in this book is to destroy the influence of the novels of chivalry, he has no need of begging maxims from philosophers, sermons from the Holy Scriptures, fables from poets, but rather he should avoid being obscure or intricate and concentrate on stirring the melancholy man to laughter, the merry to greater merriment, and not bore the simpleton. If the author succeeds in overthrowing the mania for these novels of chivalry, he will have accomplished no little thing.

All of these elements which Cervantes rejected as being vain and ridiculous, Lope de Vega had constantly used in his works, from boasting of his own noble ancestry and that of his noble protectors, to the pedantic quotations from classic Greek and Latin authors. In a literary society so aware of what was being written, these references were sufficient to move to hilarity all of those who hated Lope, and even his admirers were not averse to listening to sarcastic comments about a man who was blessed with so much.

At other times Cervantes was more precise in his attacks against Lope. He severely criticizes his rival, who, although being very well acquainted with Aristotelian rules of drama, chose to disregard them completely. These classical unities (according to Aristotle in his *Poetics*) state that in drama there should be: 1) unity of time; the action of the work should take place during a maximum time of twenty-four hours; 2) unity of action—that is, one principal plot, excluding irrelevant episodes or subplots; 3) unity of place, meaning that only one set may be used (or, interpreted more literally, that the action remain within a single general vicinity). Lope rejected these restraints at will, for he well understood the impossibility of constructing interesting plays within these limitations. In Chapter

"By touching upon this subject, Sir Canon," said the curate at this point, "you awaken in me an old grudge against the plays they are producing today. It is equal to that which I hold against the books of chivalry. For, according to Tully, drama should be a mirror of human life, an example of manners, an image of truth. However, those that are staged nowadays are mirrors of absurdity, examples of stupidity and images of lewdness. For what greater absurdity can there be in the subject at hand, than for a child to appear in the first act in swaddling clothes, and in the second act come out as a bearded man? And what more ridiculous than depict for us an old man acting the valiant, the youth who plays the coward, the eloquent lackey, or a page who gives counsel, the king as a porter and a princess in the role of a kitchen maid? And what shall I say of their manner of observing the time and the place in which the action takes place? I have seen a play whose first act took place in Europe, the second in Asia, and its third ended in Africa. If there had been a fourth act it would have finished in America, thus encompassing the four quarters of the earth. And if imitation of life is the principal element of the drama, how is it possible to satisfy the most mediocre intelligence, when the action is supposed to take place in the days of King Pepin and Charlemagne, yet whose leading character is the Emperor Heraclius, who enters Jerusalem bearing the Holy Cross and recovers the Holy Sepulcher, like Godefroi de Bouillon, although ages have passed between one event and the other? And when the comedy is based on fiction, they insert historical facts and mix with them parts of other incidents that happened to different persons at different times, and this with no attempt at verisimilitude, but with obvious errors that are absolutely inexcusable. The worst of it is that there are ignorant persons who say this is the perfect thing, and all the rest is looking for over-refinements. And if we consider sacred dramas? How many false miracles they represent! What apocryphal and erroneous incidents, attributing the miracles worked by one saint to another! And even in their comedies, dealing with earthly themes, they dare to present miracles without any motive for it, merely because they think stage effects, as they call them, will lure the ignorant public into the theater to marvel. All of this is prejudicial to the truth, detrimental to history, and casts opprobrium upon Spanish genius, because the foreigners scrupulously observe the rules of unity in their plays, and will take us for untutored barbarians when they see the nonsense and absurdities in our plays. It is sufficient to excuse all of this by saying that the main objective of well-ordered countries who permit comedies to be given in public is to entertain the common people with a little honest pastime and thereby divert the evil impulses that idleness often engenders, and that this is accomplished with any kind of a comedy, good or bad, therefore it is rather pointless to impose rules to govern the playwrights and actors of such plays, since, as I have said, they achieve this with any kind of a play."

Cervantes seemed intent upon destroying Lope's entire works, proposing at this point practically a complete censorship which would have obliged writers to bring forth dramas which moralized. Fortunately, the government paid little attention to those suggestions. Had they been followed, there would have been no Spanish theater of the seventeenth century. In the same chapter Cervantes goes on:

"All of these evils, and even more which I shall not mention, would cease if there were some intelligent and judicious person in the court who would examine all plays before they are produced, not only those that are to be acted in the capital, but all of them to be performed in other parts of Spain as well; without the approval, seal and signature of that person, no local magistrate in any town would permit any comedy to be put on. In this way the actor-managers would be careful to send their plays to Madrid to be examined, and would be able to produce them with safety. And the authors too would compose them with more care and study, fearful of the rigorous examination which their works had to pass in the hands of a competent person; and in this manner they would produce good comedies, and thus successfully achieve their objective: the entertainment of the people, at the same time enhancing the reputation of Spanish writers, and the interest and security of the actors, and save the trouble of chastising them. And if this official, or some other, were to examine the books of chivalry to be written in the future, doubtless some would appear with that perfection you have spoken of, enriching our language with the precious treasure of eloquence, overshadowing the old books by the light of the new ones. They would offer honest pastime not only for the idle, but also for the busiest persons, for our frail human condition cannot carry on without some lawful recreation." [5]

Lope became furious with these allusions from the *Quixote*. When the novel was still at the publisher's, perhaps an advance copy was circulating, for Lope wrote to the Duke of Sessa, speaking of poets: "There is none so bad as Cervantes; nor is anyone so idiotic as to praise his *Don Quixote*." Another time in the most scurrilous verses imaginable, he sought to avenge himself by referring to Cervantes' hand paralyzed in battle as an order from Heaven to keep him from writing, commenting on the great novel and its author in violent and brutal terms; in short, a most lamentable outburst. Naturally Lope's growing indignation was the result of the great numbers of readers which the *Quixote* already enjoyed.

As a matter of fact, when it appeared, its success was immediate and tremendous. The first edition licensed for the press came out in Castile in January, 1605, and sold with astounding rapidity for eight reales and twelve mara-

vedis (today worth about 100 pesetas or $1.67) in the
paper edition. Bound, it cost twelve reales (about 150
pesetas or $2.50). Its protagonists quickly entered the vo-
cabulary of the people. When Lord Charles Howard of
Effingham arrived in Madrid to put the seal on the peace
treaty between the former enemy countries, Spain and
England, Góngora composed a satirical sonnet for the
occasion, giving vent to his feelings: "The Queen gave
birth, the Lutheran arrived with six hundred heretics in his
train." He goes on to comment on the money gaily squandered to fete the man with munificent presents, jousts,
sumptuous feasts, and wine to honor the "Queen by the
grace of Calvin, and all her spies," and ends with:

> We are left poor, the Lutheran grows rich
> and those called forth to write these exploits
> are Don Quixote, Sancho and his ass.

The popularity of the work inspired endless anecdotes.
In America two years after the publication of the *Quixote*,
there appeared in a carnival masquerade a character repre-
senting Don Quixote and another playing Sancho. It was
said that King Philip III, upon seeing a man laughing heart-
ily on a street corner, with a book in his hand, said, "Either
he is mad or he is reading the *Quixote*."

A clandestine edition appeared in Valencia, taking advantage of the license which had been granted solely for
publication in Castile and Portugal. Another pirated edition came out in Lisbon, and later still another in Valencia.
It was success to the point of theft. No one steals the
unwanted! Cervantes was suddenly transformed into the
most popular of writers. His literary creations were al-

ready in the minds of the Spaniards, serving—as they would serve for three centuries—as the basis for physical and moral comparisons: to behave like Don Quixote, or to talk like Sancho Panza, and so on.

If money had not yet arrived, Cervantes had realized one aspiration. He had become famous. One of the injustices had finally been amended. Cervantes had triumphed.

How long would a triumph endure in the life of Cervantes? As in his first stirrings as a poet who was noticed in the capital, as upon his return to Spain after Lepanto, as upon his emergence as a playwright, fate always permitted him to reach the summit only to topple him immediately. Because in this happy year of 1605 occurred the strange, sordid story of Gaspar de Ezpeleta.

It took place in Valladolid, where Cervantes was then living because that city had become the capital. It was not the austere court of Philip II. His son, Philip III, discharged his official duties as a religious monarch, but the continuous parties and balls permitted a libidinous gaiety that had never been seen before. The most astonishing freedom was observed among the married women of those days, and their husbands granted them the widest range of concessions. The Count of Siruela noted: "What do the gallants want with my wife with those skinny legs of hers?" Among the gentlemen of the time, conditioned to a licentious style of life between their debts and their women, was one Gaspar de Ezpeleta.

One night Cervantes heard sounds of swords clashing and loud cries for help. He went out to the street and discovered Ezpeleta wounded. The writer and a neighbor boy carried him into the apartment next door to that of Cervantes, where the latter lived with his sisters, Magdalena and Andrea; Costanza, the illegitimate daughter of Andrea; and his own daughter, Isabel. (His wife was in Esquivias, as usual on the margin of his life during good times as well as in bad times.) The magistrate arrived and made investigations. The victim's personality was well known in the city, and dueling was prohibited. Rumors were rampant. Who could have wounded him and why? Gaspar de Ezpeleta, like so many Spaniards of that time and of the present, died better than he had lived; to the questions put to him by the magistrate, he replied vaguely so as not to compromise anyone. The officials probed in vain. Was it a question of a love affair? Yes. He nobly affirmed that it had been a legitimate duel and not an attack without risk. Just as nobly, he refused to name the lady who was the motive of the quarrel. When he died two days later, he carried the secret to the grave.

The judge made further investigations and searches. In Cervantes' apartment he found a silk dress that Ezpeleta had given to the author's sister, Magdalena, perhaps in gratitude for the care she had given him during his last hours. The declarations made by the neighbors, especially by one of them, were malicious. It was said that men entered the Cervantes' house at strange hours, and perhaps Ezpeleta himself had been among them. Such suspicions were all the judge needed to send Cervantes and all of the members of his family to jail—the same jail where his father and grandfather had gone because of their debts. Now he was there on a more serious charge, that of being an accomplice to a murder. Let us remember that, counting Algiers, this was the fourth time he had been imprisoned; it was also the fourth time, including his fateful duel in Madrid, that he had been brought before the courts of his own country.

The accusations were so vague that all of the Cervantes family were released within the month, but confined to their house. This restriction was also lifted within a few days. Thus ended another of the indignities suffered by our gentleman every time destiny began to smile upon him.

Meanwhile the book continued to enjoy a prodigious sale. A second legitimate edition came out in Valencia, and another, pirated, in the same city. An English translation appeared in 1607, after having been previously published in Brussels in Castilian (as it had been in Milan and Flanders because those countries were under Spanish domination). Money was coming in, although not in the quantity that the author hoped for, because of the pirated editions and the difficulty of collecting the money due him. Finally, in 1608, Cervantes was able to pay off the last 2,400 reales that were still charged against him from his commissary days. It seemed that along with the last debt he was also liquidating his hapless past and that henceforth everything would be felicitous.

As always, success came accompanied by unpleasantness, this time within the family. His daughter Isabel was going to be married, and Doña Catalina de Palacios, in a generous and moving gesture, came from Esquivias to sponsor the bride. The wedding took place in Madrid, to which the court had returned in 1606—and with it, Cervantes. Isabel de Saavedra showed from the first a restlessness which was not in keeping with the honest woman her father should have liked to have had in his house. Perhaps it had been the example of Andrea and her love life unblessed by the church, but it was surely one more punishment to Cervantes' sensibility, for in a short time tongues were wagging in Madrid about the adulterous affair between Isabel de Saavedra and Juan de Urbina.

Otherwise his prestige was increasing. In 1609 Cervantes joined a religious brotherhood, the Congregation of the Unworthy Slaves of the Most Holy Sacrament. This pious fraternity, in spite of its humble name, carried with it a certain air of social importance. Later, in 1612, he frequented the Sylvan Academy, a literary circle attended by some of Spain's leading writers. Whom should he run into here but Lope de Vega, who was to relate to the Duke of Sessa that in order to read some verses there, he had borrowed Cervantes' spectacles for a moment and that "they looked like two fried eggs." It was the same mocking and sarcastic Lope. Cervantes, modest in everything, could not have possessed elegant eyeglasses, for he was not elegant himself, nor would he ever be.

But how did Cervantes manage to maintain that inferiority complex in respect to Lope? For if, indeed, it is a fact that the latter kept his reputation as lord and master of Spanish theater, it is no less certain that the success of the *Quixote* had permeated all levels of Spanish society and had also crossed national boundaries into England and France, where Lope's fame would arrive only much later as he was too thoroughly Spanish to be international. Was it not time for them to view each other as equals? Or better, should not Cervantes have looked at Lope from above?

But he did not. The literary taste of the period explains that anomaly. If, as we have seen, poetry was the queen of letters, invading all segments from the personal letter to the theater, the novel, then in its beginnings, was considered purely as entertainment. The most popular literary works of the times (more so even than the theater, because they reached every corner of Spain) were the novels of chivalry which, born in the middle of the fifteenth century, had, a century later, erupted into every household. This general popularity is mentioned in the *Quixote* itself. The knight, endowed with every virtue, handsome, manly, valiant, generous, and noble, struggled fiercely to rescue the oppressed from evil, which was personified by giants, dwarfs, the cunning, and sorcerers. It was a mixture of love and bravery, forces of good against those of evil, which through the centuries has captivated the masses. In a way it was a combination similar to that of today's radio serials, or "soap operas," and Western films or novels. Like the radio serials, these novels have elements of sentimentality and suspense from one chapter to the next. They resemble the Westerns in that the protagonist is as brave as he is timid, to the point of relegating the amorous overtures to the lady, such as in the case of Oriana with Amadís. This Amadís, the most popular of the knights, produced such a commotion by his death in the book, that a gentleman, upon encountering a family weeping copiously, asked what calamity had overtaken them, and they answered that their favorite hero, Amadís de Gaula, had died. The author or authors naturally hurried to find him heirs, brothers or sons who might maintain the interest of the public. Cervantes describes these reactions in the first part of *Don Quixote*:

And as the Curate said that reading romances of chivalry had turned Don Quixote's head, the Innkeeper affirmed:

"I don't know how that can be, for in truth, as I see it, there is no better reading in the world, and I have two or three of them here along with other papers, which truly have been a boon to me, as well as to many others. At harvest time, many reapers get together here and there is always someone who knows how to read, who takes up one of those books, and some thirty of us sit around him listening with such pleasure that it keeps away a thousand gray hairs. For my part at least, when I hear tell of those frenzied and terrible blows that the knights bestow, I feel like doing the same, and I could go on listening to them night and day."

"I feel the same way," said the Innkeeper's wife, "for I never have a peaceful moment in my house except when you are listening to the reading, for then you are so carried away that you forget to scold me."

"That is the truth," said Maritornes. "Honestly I too love to hear of those delightful things, especially when they tell about the young lady lying under the orange trees in the arms of her knight, and the duenna keeping guard for them, dying of envy and in a twitter. I tell you all this is like honey!"

"And what do you think of it, young lady?" the Curate asked of the Innkeeper's daughter."

"I don't know, Father," she replied. "I too listen to them, and although I don't understand, I love to hear them. I don't like the blows that my father enjoys, but the lamentations the knights make when they are absent from their ladies sometimes make me weep with the compassion I feel for them."

"Then would you remedy their laments, young lady," asked Dorotea, "if they wept for you?"

"I don't know what I would do," replied the lass. "I know only that there are some ladies so cruel that their knights call them tigresses, lionesses and a thousand other foul names. And Heavens! I don't know what kind of people are so heartless and unfeeling as to let an honest man die or go mad rather than give him a look. I don't understand such coyness. If they are honest women, why don't they marry them, seeing that the men want nothing else?"

"Watch your tongue, miss," said the Innkeeper's wife. "You seem to know a great deal about these things. It is not proper that young ladies know nor talk so much!"

Apart from that eagerness of the young girls to inform themselves of the passionate loves of the knights-errant, there prevailed among the men a certainty that such types had existed.

The greater part of the uncultivated people firmly believed in the truth of the books of chivalry in the same way that a youngster of today accepts the prodigious exploits of a Flash Gordon. So the Innkeeper defended his library against the Curate's intent to destroy it in the name of reason. One of the motives of Innkeeper, like those of the people, for believing in those books, was based on the certainty that His Majesty's government, protector of public morality, would never have allowed such works to have been published had they not been true. And the Innkeeper failed to be impressed when the Curate tried to explain to him the memorable deeds of García de Paredes and of the Cid. In those days there was a rather flexible attitude toward historic fact, and incredible adventures were credited to authentic persons, such as when the Cid sliced his Moorish enemy in half, or when García de Paredes fought single-handed against an entire army, and other examples, such as the following from the *Quixote*:

"Well now," said the Curate, "Landlord, bring me those books. I should like to see them."

"Gladly," he responded.

And going into his room, he brought a little old trunk, fastened with a small chain, and opening it, he took out three large books and some manuscripts written in a very good hand. The first book he opened was *Don Cirongilio of Thrace*, the second *Felixmarte de Hircania*, then *The History of the Great Captain Gonzalo Hernandez of Cordoba* along with *The Life of Don Diego García de Paredes*. As the Curate read the titles of the first two, he turned his face to the Barber and said:

"Now we should have here Don Quixote's housekeeper and his niece."

"We don't need them," replied the Barber. "I know how to carry them out into the yard or put them in the fireplace, indeed there is a very good fire burning there right now."

"You mean you want to burn my books?" asked the Innkeeper.

"Just these two," said the Curate, "the one of *Don Cirongilio* and that one about Felixmarte."

"Perhaps," said the Innkeeper, "my books are heretic or phlegmatic."

"Schismatic, you mean, my friend," said the Barber, "not phlegmatic."

"All right," replied the Innkeeper, "but if you want to burn any, let it be this one about the Great Captain and the one about Diego García. I would rather a child of mine be burnt before either of the others."

"My good man," said the Curate, "those books are full of lies, nonsense and absurdities, but this one about the Great Captain is true history and tells of the deeds of Gonzalo Hernández de Córdoba, who, because of his numerous and great exploits, merited to be called by all of the world, the Great Captain, glorious epithet that he alone deserved; and this Diego de Paredes was a noble gentleman, born in the city of Trujillo in Extremadura. He was a most valiant soldier and of such physical strength that he stopped with one finger a mill wheel revolving at full speed. And another time, armed with a broadsword, standing at the entrance to a bridge, he stopped an entire vast army from entering. He did many other such things which if he had not described them himself, with the modesty of a knight who is his own historian, and had another written of them freely and dispassionately, his exploits would have cast into oblivion those of the Hectors, Achilleses and Rolands."

"Tell that one to my father," said the Innkeeper. "Is that all it takes to astonish you? Stopping a mill wheel with a finger? Good Lord, you should read what I read about Felixmarte de Hircania; in a single backhand he slashed five giants in two at the waist, as though they had been the toy friars the children make out of string beans. Another time he assaulted a vast and enormously powerful army of one million six hundred thousand soldiers, all in armor from head to foot and dispelled them all as if they had been a flock of sheep. And what about that good man, Don Cirongilio of Thrace, who, according to the book, was so dauntless and bold, that when he was sailing up a river, a fiery serpent came up from the water, and he had no sooner seen it than he threw himself astride its scaly shoulders, and with both hands choked it with such force, that the serpent, seeing that it was going to drown, had no choice but to dive to the bottom of the river, still carrying the knight who refused to let go. And when they reached the bottom he found himself in a most marvelous world of palaces and gardens. Then the serpent changed into an old man who told him the most fantastic tales. I tell you, sir, if you heard that book read aloud you would go crazy with pleasure. I would not give two figs for your Great Captain or that Diego García!"

Upon hearing this, Dorotea whispered to Cardenio: "It would take very little to make him a second Don Quixote."

"I do think so," replied Cardenio, "for from every indication, he takes every word written in those books as gospel truth and not even the barefoot friars could make him believe otherwise."

"Look here, my friend," replied the Curate, "there never was in the world a Felixmarte de Hircania, nor Don Cirongilio of Thrace, nor any such knights as those described in the romances of chivalry, because all of them are fictitious inventions of the idle minds which compose them for the purpose, as you have said, to pass the time as your reapers do in reading them. I swear to you that there never were such knights in the world, nor did such foolish exploits take place."

"Toss that bone to another dog!" replied the Innkeeper. "As if I didn't know how many make five, and where the shoe pinches. Don't feed me that pap. I wasn't born yesterday. You're a good one to try to convince me that these good books are full of absurdities and lies, for they were printed with the license of the lords of the Royal Counsel, as if they were people who would allow so many lies to be printed along with so many battles, so many enchantments as to drive a man crazy!"

A modern-day version of such exploits, although somewhat less exaggerated, is found in the deeds of the hero of the Western films, who single-handedly finishes off a band of outlaws of incredibly bad marksmanship, while all of his shots hit their mark. Even the pistol is miraculous, for it never runs out of bullets.

Well then, that was the kind of novel that was considered the prototype of narrative literature. When the *Quixote* appeared, it created as much enthusiasm among the masses as among more cultured persons. However, the latter still considered the novel an inferior literary form. It did not enjoy the prestige that it does today. Esteem for the novel as a literary form began with the *Quixote*, the first great novel of modern times. Cervantes' contemporaries did not perceive the immense philosophy of the *Quixote;* they saw in it no more than a highly successful attempt to satirize a literary form which enraptured the uncultivated masses. To this extent and no further did they concede its importance. For the intellectuals of the epoch, one single sonnet by Góngora, the most respected of the poets, was worth much more than the fifty-two chapters of the *Quixote*. Cervantes had succeeded in gaining the applause of the common people, but he was denied it by the learned.

The year 1609 was one of great commotion in Spain. The Moriscos—the only people of foreign origin living in Spain after the expulsion of the Jews, descendants of those Moors of Granada who were the last to cede their kingdom to the Spanish—were being expelled from their native land.

A minority of Spaniards, particularly the landowning nobles, tried, without success, to stop the order of expulsion—indeed for a selfish reason, because the Moriscos were their most skilled farm laborers. Later Cervantes, in one of his exemplary novels, *The Dog's Colloquy*, would state his opinion, which was in accord with that of the majority:

". . . and leaving Granada, I strayed into a garden owned by a Morisco, who welcomed me with much good will, and I was happy to stay, as I figured that protecting his garden was all he would require of me, a job, in my opinion that would be less work than that of guarding sheep, and as there was no quarrel as far as the salary was concerned, it was easy for the Morisco to find a servant to command, and for me, a master to serve. I stayed with him over a month, not because I enjoyed such life, but because I was able to learn about my master's way of life and thereby that of all the Moriscos living in Spain. Oh what things I could tell you, friend Scipio, about that Moorish riff-raff, if I were not afraid that I could not finish my story in two weeks! If I were to give all the details, I would not tell it all in two months. However, I have to tell you something, so listen to the general idea of what I saw and particularly noted in those good people. It would be a miracle to find among all of them, one person who sincerely believes in the sacred law of

Christianity; their only objective is to make money, and to hoard it, once they get it, and to do so they work and do not eat. Whenever any money comes into their hands, unless it is completely without value, they condemn it to perpetual imprisonment and eternal darkness. Thus, always earning and never spending, they have managed to amass the greater part of the money that there is in Spain. They are its money bank, its moths, its magpies, its weasels. They get everything, they hide everything, and they swallow everything. Consider the great number of them, and that every day they earn and hide a little or a lot, and that a slow fever consumes life as surely as an intense one; and as they go on increasing, they continue to augment their hoard; they multiply and will go on multiplying to infinity as experience shows. There is no chastity among them, neither men nor women take monastic vows, everyone marries, they all increase in number, because the frugal life heightens fertility. They are not consumed by wars nor by occupations which overwork them. They quietly rob us, and with the fruits of our patrimony, which they sell back to us, they become rich. They do not keep servants, for they do everything themselves; they waste no money on schools for their children, for their only science is to rob us. Of Jacob's twelve sons who, I have heard said, went into Egypt, there resulted six hundred thousand men, not counting women and children, when Moses led them out of that captivity. From this you can imagine how the wives of these will multiply, for they are incomparably greater in number.

"A remedy has been sought for all the evils you have noted and outlined; I know indeed that those you have not mentioned are more numerous and more serious than those you have told me about, and up to now, no suitable solution has been found. But our republic has extremely prudent guardians, who, considering that Spain fosters and keeps in her bosom such vipers as the Moriscos, will, with God's help, find a prompt and sure solution for such an evil."

One supposes that the author is referring to the period

before the expulsion. When it does occur, Cervantes makes known the justice of the decree through the mouth of the Morisco, Ricote. The Morisco minority constituted something of a "fifth column" within the bosom of Spanish society. Although there were good people among them, the majority were anti-Spanish and anti-Catholic, and, in case of a Turkish or Berber invasion of the peninsula, doubtlessly they would have aided the enemy.

In various chapters of the *Quixote*, Cervantes refers to the banishment of the Moriscos. In the following passage, we listen to Ricote, a Moorish shopkeeper who has been forced to flee from Spain and who has returned furtively to get a gold hoard which he has left buried outside the village:

"Well you know, oh, Sancho Panza, my friend and neighbor, what terror in all of us was caused by the edict . . . of expulsion that His Majesty proclaimed against my people. I was compelled to believe in the truth of the ruinous intentions of my race, and it was in my opinion a divine inspiration which prompted His Majesty to put into effect so gallant a resolution. Not that all of us were guilty, some of us were true and steadfast Christians, but we were so few in number that we were unable to oppose those who were not, and it was not safe for Spain to nurture the serpent within her bosom, retaining enemies from within. Finally, and with good reason, we were punished by the penalty of banishment. To some it might be considered a gentle and indulgent fate, but to us it was the most calamitous thing that they could inflict upon us. Wherever in the world we are, we weep for Spain. After all, we were born there; it is our fatherland."

Later in the novel, there is a discussion about how to arrange for Ricote and his daughter, converted Moriscos and true Christians, to remain in Spain. It is suggested that such a problem could be solved at court by favors and bribes. Ricote is opposed, feeling there is nothing to hope for from favors or bribes, and says:

". . . for the great Bernardino de Velasco, Count of Salazar, whom His Majesty has put in charge of our expulsion will not be influenced by prayers, promises, gifts, nor pity; for although it is a fact that he combines justice with mercy, he views the entire body of our race as contaminated and rotten. Therefore his cure is to amputate rather than to apply a more gentle remedy. And so with prudence, wisdom, diligence, and the terror he inspires his strong shoulders bear the burden of the execution of that royal decree. Our efforts, stratagems, petitions and tricks are all useless to distract his Argus eyes, always on the alert. Not one of our race remains concealed to later sprout, like a hidden root, and bear poisoned fruit in Spain, now cleansed, now freed from the terrors which our numbers caused her. What a heroic decision of Philip III, and what unheard of wisdom to have entrusted such a project to Don Bernardo de Velasco."

For Cervantes, life went on, bringing him yet another deception. His protector, the Count of Lemos, was named viceroy of Naples, and the novelist dreamed of accompanying him to Italy as a member of his entourage, perhaps to see his son Promontorio and to relive some of those happy Italian times. But it was not in his destiny that he should leave Madrid. Cervantes was rejected in favor of the Argensola brothers.

1610. The *Quixote* had gone through ten editions, counting the one published in Spanish in Milan (three in Madrid, three in Lisbon, two in Valencia, one in Brussels), but its author was still without funds even to the point that when his sister Magdalena died, her funeral expenses were paid by a religious order.

Cervantes ironically comments (in the second part of *Don Quixote*) on the difficulty of collecting money for his copyrights:

"But tell me, sir, this book, are you having it printed at your own expense or have you sold the copyright to some bookseller?"

"I am having it printed on my own," replied the author, "and I expect to clear a thousand ducats on it at least, from the first edition of two thousand copies. At six reales each they will be sold out in a jiffy."

"You are very apt, sir, in your calculations," answered Don Quixote. "But it seems indeed that you know little of the hocus-pocus that goes on among publishers, nor of the arrangements they make with each other. I promise you that when you see yourself encumbered with two thousand copies of the book you will find the load so heavy it will frighten you, and even more so if the book is a bit irregular and not at all racy."

"So what would you have me do, sir?" asked the author. "You would like me to give it to a bookseller who will give me three maravedis for the copyright, insisting he does me a favor by giving them to me? I am not having my books printed to achieve a reputation in the world. I am already known by my works. It is profit I am after; without it, fame is worthless."

"May God grant you good luck, sir," replied Don Quixote.

Cervantes had begun the second part of the *Quixote*, but he interrupted this work to attempt the theater once more. It seemed he was to be paid fifty ducats for each play, but they were not produced at the time, and he was to publish them four years later. As he says in the Prologue to *Interludes*:

. . . Some years ago, I returned to my former pastime, and thinking it was still the same world that once sang my praises, I again composed a few plays, but I found no birds in last year's nests. I mean I found no producers who wanted them, although they knew that I had them, so I put them away in a chest, consecrating and condemning them to eternal silence. In time a bookseller told me he might buy them from me if a properly licensed stage-manager had not told him that much could be expected from my prose but from my verse, nothing. If the truth were known, it pained me greatly to hear it and I said to myself, either I have changed into another person, or the times have changed for much the better. It is usually the other way around, for the people always praise the days that are past! I again glanced through my comedies and through some interludes of mine that had been put away with them and I decided that none of them were so bad but what they merited to come out from the darkness where that smart stage-manager had sent them, and be brought to the attention of other producers who were not so particular and who were more understanding. I wearied of it all and sold them to this bookseller who has published them as you see them here. He paid me a reasonable sum and I took the money calmly with no more tedious discussions with actors and managers. I should wish that they were the best in the world, or at least reasonably good. You will judge, dear reader, and if you find anything good in them, tell that slanderous stage-manager of mine, when you run onto him, to amend his criticism, for I offend no one; and inform him that they contain no out and out stupidities. The verse is that which these comedies demand, low style among the three possible styles. The language of the interludes is appropriate to the characters presented in them. If he amends his opinion to all of this, I shall offer him a comedy which I am in the process of writing, called *The Obvious Deception*, which, unless I am mistaken, should make him happy. And with this, may God give you health and me patience.

Interludes are an indication of what Cervantes might have done in the theater had he not clashed with an insuperable barrier in the person of Lope de Vega. All of the most diverse types of the epoch make their appearance in these plays. The soldier of *The Watchful Guard* is a relative of the squire in *Lazarillo de Tormes*. It is a description of a man with whom the author was well acquainted, the returned soldier, laden with glory but penniless, who waits for years (as the author knew at first hand) for his country to reward him for his services. In *The Miracle Show* he ironically comments on the honor complex of Spain in those days. Here an actor-manager arrives in a town and says that his theatrical troop can offer the greatest spectacle in the world, but the only ones who will be able to see it are those who were born in wedlock and have no taint of Moorish or Jewish blood in their veins. All of the villagers, convinced that they are in possession of both requirements, present themselves at the performance, where the manager announces that they will present a dancer, a flood, and a lion, none of which of course really appears.

None of those present at the performance sees anything, but no one will admit it. Everyone looks around, frightened and saddened to be the only one who does not appreciate the spectacle, but each conceals this fact and by his exclamations pretends to be enjoying it. Finally an army quartermaster comes in, asking the townspeople to make up lodgings immediately for his soldiers. He screams that there is nothing on the stage. Everyone in the audience jeers at him, repeating that he is one of the dishonored ones since he sees nothing. Angrily he breaks up the performance while the actor-manager makes a hasty getaway with the money he has swindled.

Cervantes touched the sore spot of one of the most serious Spanish problems of the time: that of the purity of their blood. A product of the sixteenth century, this complex of incredible pride extended to the most humble of

Spaniards if he could boast that in his veins flowed no blood of his religious enemies. In reality, "purity of blood" was more likely to be encountered among the peasants, who were bound to the land and who married among themselves, than among the noble class, who had frequently forgotten their principles, marrying daughters of rich Jews.

Limpieza de sangre, or purity of blood, was not just a problem of prestige or elegance. The laws of the time made the people give proof of it in order to be eligible to obtain various positions, to qualify to go to America, or to receive titles of nobility, although there were various stratagems employed to overcome the last requirement. Cervantes himself had to prove it when he aspired to a government position. His father testified in a formal document in 1569 that Miguel de Cervantes was his legitimate son and that of his lawful wife, Doña Leonor de Cortinas, and that neither he nor his son, nor said wife, nor his parents, nor his grandparents, nor those of his wife had been, or were, Moors or Jewish converts; they had never appeared before the Holy Office of the Inquisition or been tried before any other court. They had been and were good "old Christians," their blood clean of any taint, and he begged to send witnesses to attest to the above.

In another interlude, *The Election of the Magistrates,* Cervantes intensifies his ridicule of religious obsession. Since the authentic religion was found only among the traditional Spaniards uncontaminated by foreign doctrines that entered the country by means of prohibited books, it followed that the less one knew, the more likely he would escape falling into heresy and its subsequent punishment. In the following conversation, Humillos, one of the four candidates for the office of mayor is questioned:

Bachiller: You are ready for the examination?

Humillos: Yes, go ahead with it.

Bachiller: Do you know how to read, Humillos?

Humillos: Certainly not, nor would anyone in my family be so crazy as to try to learn that nonsense that sends men to the stake and women to the whorehouse. No, I don't know how to read; but I know plenty of other things that are much better than reading.

Bachiller: What kind of things?

Humillos: I know all of my prayers by heart and I pray them four or five times each week.

Rana: And with that you expect to become mayor?

Humillos: With that, and with being of pure-blood old Christian stock, I would dare to be a Roman senator.

Or to return to *The Miracle Show*:

Chanfalla: You are wrong to be dissatisfied with the musician. Really, sir, he is a very fine Christian and a well-bred nobleman besides.

Governor: Qualities so essential in a first-rate musician.

We must not forget that in the national experience of Cervantes, those theories of racial superiority carried the country from the highest pinnacle of glory to disaster. The great principles that brought the Reconquest to its conclusion and inspired the valor of Lepanto had now been converted into pure appearance, stripped of all effectiveness. The country was drowning in its cult of formalism, that is to say, in its insistence on outward forms and customs. And in his personal experience, Cervantes believed, and with reason, that he had been unjustly treated by the country and its government. He felt that something did not function in a nation which dealt thus with its most renowned men.

Was it possible that he could still be so poor? Around 1612, he wrote *Journey to Parnassus*,[6] in which Mercury has invited him to an assembly of the greatest Spanish poets. Cervantes has no seat, and Apollo tells him to fold his cloak and sit upon it, to which our poet replies, "My lord, I fear that you have not noticed that I possess no cloak." Apollo answers, "No matter, I am happy to see you here, for virtue is the cloak with which poverty clothes herself to hide her shame, and therefore envy passes her by." Cervantes' answer is: "I bowed my head before the court of Fame and remained standing, for one has no claim to a good seat unless wealth and favor have won it for him."

What bitterness in these words of a creative genius who has to his credit ten editions of the immortal *Quixote*! The physical heroism exhibited at Lepanto and in Algiers, the intellectual value demonstrated as a poet, a playwright, a novelist, were not enough to assure him a sustained income sufficient to provide him a reasonably comfortable existence removed from the anguished phantom of debts which had pursued him since his childhood.

He expressed the same bitterness when he looked for intellectual reward in the form of literary recognition from his colleagues, such as Lope de Vega and Góngora. But the literary magnates ignored him. The prologue to the *Exemplary Novels*, published in 1613, reveals once more his resentment in not attaining the favor of the well-known writers. He concludes it with, "May God protect you and give me the patience to endure the ill that many starchy hypercritics will have to say of me."

He knew that among that select group no one was going to get excited over his latest publication, the *Exemplary Novels*, which were written for entertainment and were the very literary form most scorned by those great poets. Into these stories Cervantes poured the memories of his intense and harried life, hoping to amuse the simple reader with adventures that might please without requiring too much mental effort. In the prologue he tells the reader that he will find nothing offensive in these tales, explaining that the amorous episodes found in some of them are so proper and well tempered by Christian propriety that they will not provoke impure thoughts in anyone who reads them. He says, "I have named them 'Exemplary' and if you consider them, there is not a one from which you may not draw a profitable example; and if it were not for enlarging on this subject, I might show you what tasty and wholesome fruit you might enjoy from all of them together, just as from each one by itself." He continues that his intent was "to make available to his countrymen, an entertainment which everyone could enjoy without threat to body or soul: that innocent recreation benefits rather than harms; people cannot always be at church, nor at prayer, nor ceaselessly at their work. Therefore the weary spirit needs repose, and for this reason avenues are planted with trees, fountains are sought out and gardens are cultivated."

In this collection of twelve short novels, Cervantes recalls the cities and scenes of his tormented past: the fabulous Seville of *Rinconete and Cortadilla*, the young rogues, witty and shameless, who were members of Monipodio's gang. The jail he knew from his own experience gave him ample opportunity to become acquainted with the characters that he would later describe. His travels as commissary furnished him occasion to study the curious and interesting world of the gypsies,[7] which is reflected in *The Little Gypsy*. Here Andrés, a young aristocrat, falls in love with Preciosa, a gypsy girl, and abandoning his home and career, he follows the gypsies and becomes one of them:

. . . during the rest of the day of Andrés' initiation as a member of the gypsy tribe, the following ceremonies took place: They cleared one of the best huts in the camp and adorned it with branches and plants. They seated Andrés on the stump of a cork tree, putting in his hands a hammer and tongs and made him do a couple of capers to the accompaniment of two guitars strummed by two gypsies. Then they bared one of his arms, and with a new silk ribbon through which they passed a stick, they gave him two gentle turns. Preciosa was present throughout all of this, and so were many other gypsy women, old ones and young girls who, some with amazement, and some with love, looked upon him. Such was the gallant demeanor of Andrés that even the men became fond of him.

In this novel Cervantes describes the gypsy customs and their morality, which was so different from that of the rest of Spain, especially in those times:

This girl, who is the flower and cream of all the beauty of the gypsies that we know of in Spain, we entrust to you, either for your wife, or for your mistress, and in this you may do whatever is most to your taste, for this free and easy life of ours is not subject to pruderies nor many formalities. Take a good look at her, and see if she pleases you, or if you notice something in her that you do not like. If so, choose among the other maidens here, the one that will best satisfy you and we will give you that one; but you must remember that once chosen, you cannot leave her for another, nor can you make advances either to married women or to the maids. We observe inviolably the law of friendship: no one covets that which belongs to another. We live free of the bitter plague of jealousy. Among us, although there is much incest, there is no adultery; and if one's wife is found to be unfaithful, or one's mistress deceitful, we do not go to the law to seek punishment; we ourselves are the judges and executioners of our wives and mistresses. We kill them and bury them in the mountains or the deserts as easily as though they were harmful animals. There is no relative to avenge them nor fathers to ask us to kill them. Ever fearful of this, they make certain to be chaste, and as I have told you, we live secure. . . . We have little that is not the common property of all, except the wife or the mistress, for we wish each woman to belong to the one that fate decreed her. Among us old age causes divorce as does death. If a man wishes, he can leave his aged wife, if he is young, and choose another who is better suited to his years. With these and other laws and statutes we live and are happy; we are lords of the fields, of the crops, of the forests, of the mountains, of the fountains and of the rivers. The mountains offer us wood free for the taking, the trees, fruit, the vines, grapes, the gardens, vegetables, the springs, water, the rivers, fish, and the preserves, game; shade from the rocks, fresh air from the hills, and houses from the caves. For us the inclemencies of the weather are breezes, the snow, refreshment, the rains, baths, thunder is music, lightning is our torches; for us the hard clods of earth are feather beds; the weather-beaten skin of our bodies serves as our impenetrable armor which defends us. Shackles do not impede our lightness of movement, ravines do not stop us, nor walls imprison us, cords do not twist our courage. . . . Between "yes" and "no" we make no distinction when it is to our advantage; we pride ourselves on being martyrs rather than confessors; for us pack animals are reared in the fields and purses are clipped in the cities. There is no eagle, nor any bird of prey who more swiftly swoops down on the victim it beholds, than we on the opportunities which offer us some gain. In short, we possess many talents which promise us a happy end, because in prison we confess, but on the rack we are silent, we work by day, and steal by night, or rather we warn people not to be careless as to where they put away their goods. We are not bothered about losing our honor, nor do we stay awake from the desire to increase it. We endure no factions, nor arise at daybreak to give memorials, nor wait upon magnates nor solicit favors. . . . We are rustic astrologers because as we nearly always sleep under the open sky, we know every hour of the day and night. . . . We turn the same face to the sun as to the frost, to famine as to plenty. In conclusion we are people who live by our industry and our wits . . . we have what we want, for we are satisfied with what we have. I have told you all of this, generous youth, so that you might not be ignorant of the life that you have chosen and the customs which you will have to profess, some of which I have outlined here, and many other things that you will discover for yourself, no less worthy of consideration than those you have just heard.

The Force of Blood relates a story of an illegitimate child, which was a popular theme of that time. *The Spanish-English Lady* was an attempt to overcome the enmity which had divided and bloodied the relations between his own country and Great Britain. Again Cervantes showed himself ahead of his time, begging for understanding and friendship among nations, in spite of their religious and national differences. In *The Dog's Colloquy*, Scipio and Berganza, from the point of view of domestic animals, discuss the current problems of mankind, ranging from education to sensuality. In *The Man of Glass* he returns to the obsession he had so lengthily developed in *Don Quixote*; the *loco-cuerdo*, or wise madman. The *licentiate* (college graduate) Tomás Rodaja's madness lies in that he believes himself made of crystal and therefore fragile and terribly in danger of being broken if touched. His mind oscillates between good and evil, between truth and error. What is right? That which appears to be so, or that which the others take for certain? And who are the others who can know what is truth for him?

Cervantes mirrors the society of the epoch in *The Deceit-*

ful Marriage. A soldier, Ensign Campuzano, marries a woman of questionable past, in order to fleece her. She, one of the many in Madrid at that time dedicated to deceiving the unwary, borrows fancy clothes and an apartment with elegant appointments, even gifts, in order to trick and humiliate him in turn.

"To this my genius has applied itself," Cervantes says in the prologue, "and in this direction my inclination leads me, and especially I am aware that I am the first to write novels in the Castilian tongue. The many novels that circulate printed in Spanish are all translated from foreign languages, while these are my own, neither imitated nor stolen. My genius engendered them, my pen gave them birth."

His resentment was tempered with a genuine awareness of his worth. He knew that he had created a new literary form in the Castilian tongue, even if the critics insisted upon discrediting the novel as inferior to poetry. Besides, who could take from him the honor of having created the personage of Don Quixote, known throughout the world? On that point it was too late to do harm to him.

Too late? In 1614 Cervantes was working on Chapter 36 of the second part of the novel when fortune shattered his castle of illusions. The greatest piracy in the literary world took place in the city of Tarragona with the appearance of *"Second Volume of the Ingenious Gentleman Don Quixote de la Mancha,* which contains his third sally and is the fifth part of his adventures, written by the Licentiate Alonso Fernández de Avellaneda, native of the town of Tordesillas."

What must Cervantes have felt upon learning this piece of news? They had robbed him of a hand at Lepanto, of his liberty in Algiers, of his honor in the jails of Seville and Valladolid, of money in the theaters of Madrid. And now they were trying to snatch away the only fruit of his creative genius that had brought him renown; the only off-spring among those he had created whose name was on everybody's lips! But the thief was not satisfied with seizing his property; he wanted to assassinate his reputation, physical as well as moral. In the prologue Avellaneda says:

Besides, Miguel de Cervantes is now as old as the castle of San Cervantes,[8] and because of his years, so dissatisfied that he is irritated with everything and everybody, and because of it, is so lacking in friends that when he wants to adorn his books with high-sounding sonnets, he has to attribute them, as he himself says,[9] to Prester John of the Indies or to the Emperor Trebizond because probably he cannot find anyone in all of Spain who would so degrade himself as to speak his name. Let him content himself with his *Galatea* and his plays in prose, which have an advantage over his novels; they do not bore us. Saint Thomas (Secundae Secundae quaestio 35) teaches that envy harms only oneself. . . . But let us excuse the errors of the First Part on the basis that it was written within the walls of a prison, and therefore could not but emerge branded by it, nor be anything else but querulous, gossipy, impatient and choleric.

Cervantes answered the author of the spurious *Quixote*:

. . . What I can not help resenting is that he chides me for being old and crippled, as if it had been in my power to stop the passage of time, or as if my hand had been maimed in some tavern, instead of during that most glorious occasion that past, present or future centuries will ever hope to see. If my wounds do not shine in the eyes of those who behold them, they are at least esteemed by those who know where I got them, for a soldier looks better dead in battle than safe in flight, and this is so ingrained in me that if it were now possible to recall that occasion, I would prefer my wounds from having fought in that prodigious action than to be without them and not to have taken part in it . . . and I should like to remind him that one does not write with gray hairs, but with the mind, which generally improves with age.

(Don Quixote, Part II, Prologue)

Who was the person who thus attacked him? In the history of Spain there are two mysteries which are closely related to the important events of her past. The first, what were the origins of Christopher Columbus, and the second, who was hiding under the name of Avellaneda? Tirso de Molina? Argensola? Ruiz de Alarcón? Various names have been suggested, but the authorship has never been proven for certain. Whoever it was must have been a close friend of Lope de Vega. The ancient rivalry again came to the surface, and there was no lack of those who affirmed that it was that very phoenix of creativity himself concealing his identity under that pseudonym. If not he, it was probably one of his greatest admirers who came forth to attack Cervantes. In his career as a novelist did he now have to confront that giant who had cut short his course in the theater?

It seemed the reason was to be found in the ironic words of the prologue to the First Part of the *Quixote*, where Cervantes ridicules the aristocratic and cultural pretensions of Lope and his works; Avellaneda insists in his prologue:

If we differ in methods it is because his choice of them is offensive to me, and particularly to the man whom the most remote nations so justly applaud, and to whom our own country owes so much for his having wholesomely and tirelessly furnished the theaters of Spain for so many years countless and splendid plays written with all of the art demanded by the public, and with the orthodoxy and purity that are expected from a minister of the Holy Office.

Cervantes acknowledges for the first time, in Chapter 59 of the Second Part, the shock he received at the publication of the apocryphal *Quixote* (he wrote the prologue last of all, as writers commonly do), and from that point on until the end of the book the author insists upon defending his protagonist, his creation, from the bogus knight. To do so he permits Don Quixote to speak out when he learns of the existence of the other book in which his character undergoes some rare changes.

The author achieves this by situating the knight at an inn, in a room whose partition is so thin he can hear a conversation in the adjoining chamber. Two gentlemen are discussing the new book and quote the author as saying that Don Quixote is no longer enamored of Dulcinea. Upon these words our knight becomes enraged and indignant and asks for an explanation. His neighbors, after recognizing him, show him the parody they are reading. Don Quixote (Cervantes) examines it, and his fury and outrage are such that he criticizes the book in no subtle terms, accusing the author of being Aragonese (an allegation which perhaps hindered rather than helped in the search for the real Avellaneda) and of giving the wrong name to Sancho's wife. The latter was something Cervantes had done several times throughout the first part. He had better reason to complain that Avellaneda's Sancho Panza is more gluttonous than humorous, as opposed to the Cervantine creation. When the real Don Quixote reads in the apocryphal work that the knight had been to Saragossa, he refuses to set foot there so that the world will see the difference between the two.

Cervantes' obsession with the new book was essentially sad. Not only did it force him to change Don Quixote's itinerary and send him to Barcelona instead of Saragossa, but from then on the knight is to continually refer to his counterpart. In Chapter 62 he sees in a book printer's shop in Barcelona a copy of the spurious work. "Upon my conscience," says the knight, "I thought that it had been burned by now and reduced to ashes for its impertinence," and he leaves the printing shop with looks of some annoyance.

But more than "some annoyance" was boiling in the blood of poor Miguel de Cervantes, struggling against time to bring out the authentic second part, which would put an end, once and for all, to the hoax. In chapter after chapter he had to return to his rival; in chapter after chapter he had to include in the thread of his story an allusion to the man who had tried to rob him of his fame and fortune. In Chapter 70 he has the maiden Altisidora standing at the gates of hell where she sees the devils tossing a book from one to another (the book is of course Avellaneda's *Don Quixote*). "Throw it into the depths of hell; may I never lay eyes on it again," said one devil. That is what Cervantes wished might happen to it, but it was not that easy to dispose of it. There it was displayed in the book stores, present in the literary commentaries, favorable or malicious, by friends and enemies. Said Don Quixote, ". . . that story goes from hand to hand, but stops in none because everyone gives it a kick."

Good or bad, liked or disliked, it went on and on, and the influence of this unknown person weighed on Cervantes' mind, impelling him to repeat a thousand and one times that he was the only author, and that his adversary's book was false. In Chapter 72 he has the authentic Quixote confronted by a gentleman, who until then had been deceived by the fraudulent knight. Our hero cries, "I am Don Quixote of La Mancha, he whom fame has celebrated, and not that miserable wretch who has usurped my name and has tried to appropriate to himself the honor of my thoughts." In reality, in reading these lines, we hear Cervantes crying, "I am Don Miguel de Cervantes, he whom fame has celebrated, and not that miserable wretch."

In the last chapter, the seventy-fourth, Cervantes makes the most desperate of decisions. Don Quixote shall die so that no one else can invent new sallies, which he, Cervantes, his only creator, does not himself conceive:

Item: I entreat the said executors that if by good fortune they happen to meet the author of a book now circulating under the title of *Second Part of the Exploits of Don Quixote de la Mancha*, that they most earnestly beg his pardon on my behalf, for my having been unintentionally the cause of his writing so many and such great absurdities as he has done; for I leave this life with sentiments of remorse that I have been the cause of his publishing such a work.

. . . And the most prudent Cide Hamete[10] said to his pen: Here you will remain hanging from this rack on this brass wire. I do not know if you are well cut or badly sharpened, here you shall live for long ages to come, unless presumptuous and wicked historians take you down to profane you. But before they touch you, warn them as best you are able

> Hands off you scoundrels!
> None shall touch you;
> For this enterprise, my good king,
> Has been kept for me alone.

For me alone Don Quixote was born, and I for him. He

knew how to act and I to write; we two alone are as one, in spite of that spurious author from Tordesillas who dared and who may dare again to take up his coarse and badly trimmed ostrich quill, to write of the exploits of my valiant knight. For this is no burden for his shoulders, nor theme for his indifferent capacity. And if by chance you should come to know him, advise him to let the weary and moldering bones of Don Quixote rest in their grave and not try to carry him off, contrary to all the laws of death, to Old Castile, making him leave the sepulcher where he really and truly lies stretched out full length, now quite powerless to make a third expedition and new sally; surely the two he did make, to the delight and approval of all who heard of them, both here and abroad, are sufficient to make a mockery of the countless knights-errant and the sallies which they undertook. In so doing, you will fulfill your Christian profession by giving good counsel to one who wishes you ill; and I shall be proud to be the first to have enjoyed the fruits of his writing, as fully as he desired, for I have no other purpose than to arouse the abhorrence of the false and absurd stories of the books of chivalry, which, thanks to this tale of my genuine Don Quixote, are already faltering and without a doubt, are doomed to extinction.

Cervantes' position can only inspire our sympathy and affection. Wounded, offended to the depths of his soul by remarks in bad taste and of malicious intent, he claims the honor of having been wounded in a glorious action, and he reminds the reader, sensibly, that the mind, like a good wine, generally improves, rather than worsens, with the years. Any reader would react in favor of the maligned, modest Miguel de Cervantes.

But Cervantes was not modest. Cervantes was very much aware of his immense worth, and several times during his literary career he spoke of himself as a profound and unique talent.

In a prefatory sonnet in the novel he has Don Quixote say through the mouth of Amadís de Gaula:

> You shall be renowned for valor.
> Your fatherland will be first among nations,
> And your learned author unique and alone in the world,

and in the dedication *To the Count of Lemos* (Second Part) he combines another attack upon the false *Quixote* with a proud assessment of himself:

> Some days past I sent to Your Excellency my plays, printed before they were produced, and if I remember correctly, I said that Don Quixote, with his boots and spurs, was ready to go and pay his respects to Your Excellency. Now I can tell you that he is booted and is on his way, and if he arrives, I believe I shall have done Your Excellency some service, because from innumerable places I have been encouraged to send him out to quell the aversion and nausea caused by another Don Quixote, who has been going about the world masquerading as the second part.

Cervantes could not tolerate that his self-assured arch-rival Lope had in turn mentioned him in his book *Pilgrim* with the motto *Velis, nolis, Invidia aut unicus aut pelegrinus* ("Like it or not, he is envious of the one and only") and had attacked him violently through his friends.

In retaliation, Cervantes strikes back harshly in a few lines further on in the same prologue. But as usual, his inferiority complex before Lope is evident. He does not name him, but by affecting admiration toward the great playwright, he pretends to refute the accusation of being anti-Lope:

> I also resent Avellaneda's calling me envious, explaining to

me, as though I am ignorant, just what envy is all about. There are two kinds, but I know only the good, the noble and well-intentioned kind. Therefore I do not have to persecute any priest, and certainly not if he is a member of the Holy Office. And if he wrote it for the person for whom it seems to be intended, he is completely mistaken, for I adore that person's genius, I admire his works and his constantly virtuous life.

All of Madrid was aware of Lope's "constantly virtuous life." In spite of having become a priest and a member of the Holy Office (of the Inquisition), his incredibly scandalous conduct, his love affairs with women inside and outside the theater, were known by all. On Saint John's day in 1614, according to a letter written by Lope himself, two confessors had refused to give him absolution and another sent him away "as angrily as if he had said he were a heretic."

Lavish in praise of poetry, Cervantes makes veiled attacks on Lope's immorality and defamatory verses. "Poetry should not be debased by writing indecent satires nor cruel sonnets," and ". . . if the poet were chaste in his habits, he will also be chaste in his verses." Even when he praises his rival's skill with one of his typical allusions, it is with irony: "Shoemaker, I know little about poetry, but your verses sound good to me—like Lope's, as all good poetry is, or appears to be." One must note "is, or appears to be." (*The Watchful Guard*)

The wide-reaching acceptance of Cervantes' masterpiece did not greatly relieve the poverty which continued to plague him. Looking again at the prologue of the Second Part, we find a dolorous but concealed lament:

. . . Tell him, too, that I could not care less about his threat to deprive me of my profit because of his book [he is still addressing Avellaneda] for I reply to him . . . long live the Count of Lemos, whose Christian charity and well-known generosity protect me against all of the blows of my paltry fortune. And long live the supreme benevolence of His Eminence of Toledo, Don Bernardo de Sandoval y Rojas. . . . These two princes, without expecting adulation or any other kind of flattery from me, have, from the goodness of their hearts, taken it upon themselves to accord me favors and kindnesses for which I consider myself happier and richer than if fortune, by her usual way, had placed me on her summit. The poor man may aspire to honor, but not the wicked. Poverty can cloud nobility, but cannot obscure it completely. If there be some light to show through virtue, even though it filter through the obstacles and cracks of poverty, it will come to be esteemed by high and noble spirits, and therefore favored.

Beautiful, elevated, worthy and so very sad are these words of the greatest writer that the Spanish centuries had seen, before the possible threat of continued penury; written not as a man self-assured concerning his work, but as being certain of his benefactors. It seems incredible that in 1614, after the fabulous success of his novel, Miguel de Cervantes had to rely more upon the generosity of an aristocrat and a prelate than on the profits which his books should logically have brought him. Cervantes does not call himself poor with the sole intention of inspiring compassion and thereby obtaining something. Because in the *Approbation* (statement by the censor at the beginning of the Second Part) the Licentiate Márquez Torres refers to the author's situation with an interesting anecdote about the astonishing fact of which Cervantes complained: that an author of such fame could be poor. After criticizing the writers who, in order to entertain their readers, fall all too easily into licentiousness and effrontery, he praises Cervantes:

. . . How differently our nation, and foreign countries as well, feel about the writings of Miguel Cervantes. They long to see this writer whom they look upon as a miracle. Because of their propriety and decency, and the suavity of their discourses, his books have been received with general applause in Spain, France, Italy, Germany and Flanders. I can state in all truth that on February 25, of this year, 1615, when His Eminence, Don Bernardo de Sandoval y Rojas, Cardinal Archbishop of Toledo, paid a return visit to His Excellency the Ambassador of France, who had come to Spain to arrange the marriages between the royal houses of France and Spain, many gentlemen of the ambassador's retinue, as courteous as they were cultured, came up to me and to other chaplains of the Cardinal, eager to know what were currently the best books in Spain, and what one was I censoring at the moment. No sooner did they hear the name Cervantes, than they began to rave and extol the author whose works were so esteemed in France and neighboring countries. They were familiar with the first part of the *Quixote* and the *Exemplary Novels*, and one of them knew most of *La Galatea* by heart. Their praise was so enthusiastic that when I offered to take them to see the author, they most eagerly accepted. They asked me many questions about his age, his profession, his background and fortune. I was obliged to tell them that he was old, a soldier, a gentleman, and poor, to which one of them replied, "How is it that Spain has not made such a man very rich, and maintained by the State Treasury?" Another of the gentlemen hastened to say with some wit, "If it is necessity that prompts him to write, may it please God to see that he never becomes wealthy, so that by remaining poor himself, he may enrich the world by his books."

I do believe that as censor, I may have gone a bit far. Some may say that my remarks border on flattery. But the truth of what I have sparingly set forth here will inform the critics and thereby ease my conscience. Besides, today no one flatters anyone who is not able to return the favor, and though such blandishments are useful, they have to be materially rewarded.

The *Second Part of the Ingenious Knight Don Quixote of La Mancha* went on sale in November, 1615. The title had undergone a slight change, from *hidalgo* (gentleman) in the first part to *caballero* (knight) in the sequel. Perhaps this was to differentiate it from the false *Quixote*.

What are the essential differences between the first and second parts? In the first place, the author has paid more attention to form in the second part. The errors for which he was reproached in the first part have disappeared, thanks to his greater care in the writing of it, and to the fact that this time it was conceived as a single story. Nearly all of the interpolated episodes have also disappeared. Cervantes had introduced them, thinking to make less tedious the narration of his hero's adventures. The critics had reproved him for this, saying that the short tales distracted from the exciting central story, and Cervantes conformed with that opinion, which naturally flattered him. He also thought, as he says:

. . . that many readers, carried away by their interest in the exploits of Don Quixote, would pay scant attention to these short tales, passing over them either hastily or with boredom, thereby failing to note their grace and fine craftsmanship, which indeed would have been quite obvious, had they been published as separate works and not attached to Don Quixote's lunacy or Sancho's nonsense. Therefore in the second part, he decided not to insert any more separate tales nor those interwoven with the narrative, but only a few episodes like them which should come up naturally in the course of events.

But the greatest difference between the two books is in Don Quixote's manner of reacting. According to the novel only a few weeks have passed when the hero undertakes his third sally, in the beginning of the second part. But according to a real calendar, nearly ten years had gone by, ten years of tribulation and distress. In spite of the success of the book, Cervantes was now past sixty, weighed down with life's problems, literary and domestic. His alter ego, Don Quixote, had to undergo the same transformation. He had become an older Don Quixote, aggrieved and, in short, weakened.

This weakness, more in spirit than in body, is noted in various aspects of his new adventures. For one thing, the person of Sancho acquires greater importance. The Squire, who in the first part was a disciplined and humble servant, becomes conceited, swells with pride, and demonstrates increasingly greater familiarity with his master, until one day he lies to him about the enchantment of Dulcinea. Later he quarrels with him, disobeys him, and in a dramatic moment, fights with him and places his knee upon his master's chest when the knight tries to force him to greater sacrifices in order to disenchant Dulcinea. As frequently occurs in life, the servant with many years of service begins to act with authority over his master, who has grown too old to impose his will as in the past. To give greater emphasis to Don Quixote's crumbling forces, Cervantes concedes greater amplitude to the personage of Sancho, even dedicating several chapters exclusively to his exploits, such as his governorship of the island of Barataria.

There are other facets to the debility of the new Don Quixote. The spirit which compels him to undertake new adventures counters a diminishing will, which prevents him from carrying them out completely. "He started to consider in what manner he could assail them with the least danger to his person," he says before the possible assault of a group of actors from the play *Parliament of Death.* And although on other occasions he recovers his former valor (his adventures with the Knight of the Mirrors and the Knight of the White Moon), the forces of the Don Quixote of former times have greatly yielded to time. Also his reactions have become less violent toward anyone who doubts that his beloved Dulcinea of Toboso was the most beautiful woman in the world. In the first part Don Quixote challenged the incredulous at once to an extraordinary battle, such as the adventure with the traders whom he threatens: "Let everyone stand where he is unless everyone will confess that the most beautiful damsel in all of the world is the Empress of La Mancha, the peerless Dulcinea of Toboso." And when one of the thus-warned merchants asks if they may not see her so as to have proof of such esthetic superiority, he indignantly tells them: "If I were to show her to you, what merit would there be in confessing a truth so evident! The important thing is that without seeing her you believe, confess, affirm, swear and defend it. Otherwise, monstrous and arrogant band, I challenge you to battle with me."

In the second part, however, when they shout, "Long live Camacho and Quiteria! He is as rich as she is beautiful and she is the most beautiful in the world," he limits himself to saying, "It is obvious that these people have never seen Dulcinea of Toboso, for if they had seen her, they would not be so lavish in their praises of this Quiteria."

But the greatest decline of the unfortunate knight is seen in his lack of faith in his own illusions. Although Don Quixote has always lived with the fear that all is illusion, and although even in the first chapter of the first part, when he has repaired the cardboard visor, he has no desire to see if it will resist another stroke of his sword, he manifests great confidence in his dreams. When harsh reality shatters his illusions, when the giants change themselves into windmills or into wine skins, there has been no error on his part. What has occurred is that enchanters and sorcerers are persecuting him; they have transformed *afterward* the object of his wrath in order to humiliate him. But in the second part, Don Quixote himself has real doubts about his magical mission to liberate the oppressed. After he has descended into Montesinos' cave and tells what he has seen there, his story seems blended with self-mockery, with materialistic elements of doubtful taste, such as Durandarte's dried and salted heart, the request for money by a maiden on behalf of Dulcinea. For the first time, it seems that Don Quixote is poking fun at what he formerly held most sacred, and when Sancho, in his turn, attempts to describe an adventure (that of the horse Clavileño), Don Quixote whispers in his ear, "Sancho, if you want me to believe what you saw up in the sky, I ask you to believe what I saw in the cave of Montesinos. And I say no more."

The defeatist melancholy that had cropped out occasionally in the first part is now encountered in all situations. Don Quixote is victim of the most unpleasant and cruel jokes precisely because those who inflict them are not ignorant muleteers or thick-shelled galley slaves incapable of appreciating the greatness of his heart, but rather some aristocrats who should have a more elevated purpose and a greater understanding of the quixotic tragedy. From Dulcinea's enchantment, invented by Sancho in the tenth chapter, Don Quixote's sadness carries him slowly toward his end. When his illusion is shattered, when he recovers his sense, Don Quixote physically dies, for he no longer has any reason to live.

Don Quixote died just one year before his creator, the difference being that the latter died at the very moment he was beginning to triumph. He had completely finished the second part of the work at the time of the momentary fame of Avellaneda's book. No one any longer disputed Cervantes' being the only and absolute master of the existence of Don Quixote of la Mancha. Also, perhaps for the first time in his life, he was viewing the future with a certain confidence. He noticed now another atmosphere among the nobles, those great gentlemen who had abandoned him for so many years, such as those mentioned in Chapter 24 of the second part:

"I should like to know, if, by the grace of God, they grant you a license to print those books (which I doubt) and to whom do you intend to dedicate them?"

"There are lords and grandees in Spain to whom they might be dedicated," said the Cousin.

"Not many," replied Don Quixote, "and not because they are undeserving of the honor, but because they do not wish to accept it, and thereby obligate themselves to materially reward the authors for their labor and courtesy."

This was an old sore spot in Cervantes' heart, having been rebuffed by the Duke of Béjar and other noblemen. But in

the following words there is a hope which was soon fulfilled: "I know a prince who can supply what all of the
others lack, with so many advantages that if I were so daring
as to enumerate them, I would arouse the envy in more
than one generous person."

That prince was probably the Count of Lemos, who
in spite of having refused to take the writer to Naples with
him, now generously rewarded him. Between him and the
Cardinals Niño de Guevara of Seville and Sandoval y
Rojas of Toledo, Cervantes at last enjoyed some economic
stability which permitted him to move into a better house
in Calle de León (Street of the Lion), and a certain domestic
tranquility in the company of his wife, who had at last left
Esquivias to live by his side and share with him that kind of
gentle understanding which, after a great many years,
sometimes comes to married couples in spite of the absence
of any profound love throughout their lives. (On the other
hand, his daughter continued to exist on the sad margin of
Cervantes' life. Juan de Urbina, her lover, had gone to
prison for debts contracted in her behalf, and Cervantes
had refused to intervene, for he was by then competely
heartbroken by her bad behavior toward him.)

For the remainder of his existence, life made up to him,
stingily but surely, what, until then, it had denied him.
In 1615, he published *Eight Plays and Eight Interludes
Never Before Presented*. Since the actor-managers had refused to put them on the stage, at least they now appeared
in printed version. He was working on the last part of *The
Trials of Persiles and Segismunda*, which would bring him
more fame even than the *Quixote*, or so he hoped. In the
prologue of this work he predicted the death that was

awaiting him and which was to prevent his seeing the first printing of the work. He wrote that as he was returning from Esquivias, a student caught up to him:

No sooner did the student hear the name Cervantes, than he got down from his horse, . . . threw himself upon me and seized me by the left hand, and exclaimed, "Yes, yes, it is the cripple who is sound, the completely famous, the joyous writer, in short, the delight of the Muses."

I, in seeing myself so extravagantly praised in so short a time, felt it would be discourteous not to respond and so said to him, "That is an error into which many of my uninformed friends have fallen, sir. I am Cervantes, but not the delight of the Muses nor any of the foolish things you have said of me. Go back and get your donkey and mount him and let us travel the little remaining distance in good conversation."

The student courteously did so, and we continued at a leisurely pace, and when the discussion touched upon my illness, the good student immediately destroyed my illusions by saying, "The disease you have is dropsy, and all of the water of the ocean won't cure you no matter how fresh you may get it. Señor Cervantes, you should drink less, but don't forget to eat, and that will cure you without any other medicine."

"Many have told me the same," I answered. "But I am so given to drinking water it is as if I were born for this alone. My life is drawing to a close, and at the rate my pulse is beating, it will end its career by this Sunday at the latest when my life will be finished. You have met me at an unfortunate moment, for I shall not have time to offer my gratitude for the good will you have shown me."

At this point we reached the bridge of Toledo, which I crossed and he went on his way. . . . What will be said about this incident my friends will enjoy relating and I shall take even greater pleasure in listening to them. We embraced each other again, he spurred his donkey, leaving me as indisposed as he was ill mounted on his donkey. He had given me a fine occasion to write some witty pages. But all times are not the same. The time will come, perhaps, when I shall pick up the broken thread and say what should be said. Farewell to all that is charming, farewell, merry friends; I am dying, and my desire is to see you soon, happy in the life to come.

All of Cervantes is in these lines, jesting or not: the certainty of his worth, of his creative talent, of his name, which would live on, even though he were to disappear. "Let me die, but long live my fame," is the Spaniard's motto in war and in letters.

The work was to go on after the physical death of its author. *The Trials of Persiles and Segismunda* he completed in April, 1616, and it was published the following year and quickly reached six editions. When he had put the finishing touches on the work, he sent it to his benefactor with a dedication that breathes a solemn peace. For the first time Cervantes does not complain of fate, for it seemed that at last he was attaining literary glory and economic well-being, after such long labors.

I might wish that those old verses, so celebrated in their time, which begin,
    With my foot already in the stirrup,
were not so appropriate to this letter, because I could begin by these very same verses saying:
    With my foot already in the stirrup,
    And the agony of death upon me,
    Great Lord, I write this to you.
Yesterday they gave me extreme unction and today I write this dedication: The time is short, my agony increases, my hopes diminish and with it all my desire to live keeps me alive. I should like to prolong it until I might pay my respects to Your Excellency! My happiness at seeing you back in Spain might give me life. But if it is decreed that I am to lose it, may God's will be done. At least Your Excellency knows my senti-

ments, and that you had in life a servant so devoted that he would go beyond death to show you his good intent.

And if by some good luck, which in my case would be a miracle, and Heaven were to grant me life, you shall see them (works in progress: *Weeks of the Garden* and *The Famous Bernardo*) and along with them the conclusion of *La Galatea*, a work which pleased Your Excellency.

He wrote this letter on April 19, 1616. Four days later he was in his last agony. Reviewing the past that he was leaving behind him, what memories must have inexorably crowded his last moments: the duel during his student days, the merry life of the soldier, the victorious battle, the chains of Algiers, the journeys through Andalusia collecting wheat and olive oil, the debtors' prison, the incarceration for complicity in a murder, the joy of his literary triumph, the wound received from Avellaneda, the sadness of such late recognition, which he was beginning to enjoy, now that he was departing forever.

At his side was the wife who had never understood him and who probably had never really loved him. His gaze fixed on the door, Cervantes waited in vain for that figure to appear who was of his flesh and blood. It was a futile wish. His daughter Isabel was not at her father's bedside when he breathed his last.

He had shortly before entered the Third Order of San Francisco. According to the rules of the Order he was carried to his grave with his face uncovered. It was as if unconsciously he had decided that some of those Spaniards who had treated him so badly in life might see him a few minutes longer, for they were to be so proud of him after death.

For me I know but this: by passion led,
    I found me chanting forth, in tercets free,
    Things which the Pontine exile never said:
"Not by the mob," quoth I, "esteemed is he
    Who follows you, my lord, and leans his back
    For rest against the laurel's sacred tree;
Envy and folly ever dog his track,
    And, envied thus and driven to distress,
    The good he hopes for he must ever lack.
I cut and fashioned by my wit the dress,
    With which fair *Galatea* sought the light,
    And left the region of forgetfulness.

I've *Comedies* composed whose style of play
    To reason so conformed, that on the stage
    They showed fair mingling of the grave and gay;
I've given in *Don Quixote*, to assuage
    The melancholy and the moping breast,
    Pastime for every mood, in every age;
I've in my *Novels* opened, for the rest,
    A way whereby the language of Castile
    May season fiction with becoming zest.

TRANSLATOR'S NOTES

1. In its origin Islam has a common source with Christianity and Judaism; however, it has no priesthood or ecclesiastical hierarchy, no altars or sacraments.

2. Janissary: a soldier (originally a slave) in the Turkish Sultan's guard, established in the fourteenth century and abolished in 1826.

3. François Villon (1431–?), pen name of François de Montcorbier, celebrated French lyric poet of the late Middle Ages. Banned from Paris for his complicity in brawls, murders, and robberies. Oscar Wilde (1856–1900), Irish-born English playwright, poet, and prose writer, as well known for his brilliant wit as for his eccentricity and affectation of behavior.

4. Castalia is a spring on Mt. Parnassus (Delphi, Greece) sacred to Apollo and the Muses. Its waters were considered to be a source of poetic inspiration.

5. Cervantes later revised this reactionary doctrine in his own eight plays, published in 1615. These followed the technique of Lope de Vega.

6. *Journey to Parnassus*, which did not appear in print until 1614, is a long satirical poem, written in triplets of unequal merit. It is most useful to the biographer, for it contains many details of Cervantes' life which are not found elsewhere. The poem is often sarcastic in tone, mentioning the poet's poverty, the lack of appreciation among his literary colleagues, his jealousy, the shabbiness of his appearance. But through it all shines Cervantes' inner serenity, his unwavering faith in his own genius.

7. The gypsies arrived in Spain in the early fifteenth century. They are thought to have originated in India and Egypt. (The name gypsy meant Egyptian.) Although they comprise an eternally nomadic race, they have developed into a sedentary society in Granada, where they live with relative permanence. They have been important interpreters, but not creators, of "flamenco" song and dance, and have frequently distinguished themselves as bullfighters.

8. San Servando in Toledo, called San Cervantes by the common people.

9. Refers to the Prologue of the First Part of *Don Quixote*.

10. Cervantes, in Chapter 9 of the First Part, establishes Cide Hamete Benengeli, an Arabic historian, as the true author of *Don Quixote*. Cervantes claims to have found and bought the manuscript in Toledo, and it is he who is having it published.

THE LITERARY WORKS
OF CERVANTES

——◄═◆═►——

1560–1567   A sonnet to Isabella of Valois.

1569   A couplet, four quatrains, a sonnet (epitaph) and an elegy in tercets of 199 verses, all of it commemorating the death of Isabella of Valois.

1575–1580   The period of the author's captivity in Algiers. Various dramatic works (lost); two sonnets, 1577, dedicated to his companion in captivity, Bartolomé Ruffino; epistle in tercets dedicated to Mateo Vázquez, Secretary of State; and twelve octets, 1579, addressed to the Sicilian poet Antonio Veneziano.

1583   A laudatory sonnet which is included in the *Romancero* of Pedro de Padilla.

1584   A sonnet to the *Austriada* by Juan Rufo, quatrains dedicated to Fra Pedro Padilla.

1585   *The First Part of the Galatea* and verses of the *Spiritual Garden* by Padilla.

1586   A sonnet and various poems in the *Cancionero* of Gabriel López Maldonado.

1588   Several theatrical works are of this period. Only the last two of the following plays have come down to us: *The Treaty of Constantinople and the Death of Selim, The Great Turquesca, Jerusalem, The Naval Battle, Amaranta, The Forest of*

Love, Arsinda, The Comedy of Confusion, The Traffic of Algiers, Numancia. In the last named the author wrote an ode which prophesied the triumph of the Invincible Armada, and shortly afterward, another, which lamented its disaster.

1591   A ballad included in *Collection of Various and New Ballads,* edited by Andrés de Villalta.

1595   Poems for the celebrations held in Saragossa in honor of Saint Jacinto. These brought him the first prize and three silver spoons.

1596   A sonnet dedicated to the Marquis Santa Cruz, printed in *Brief Compendium of Commentary on Military Discipline* by Cristobal Mosquera de Figueroa, and the famous satirical sonnet dedicated to the entry of the Duke of Medina Sindonia into Cadiz after it had been sacked and evacuated by the Earl of Essex.

1597   A sonnet commemorating the death of the poet Herrera.

1598   Poems and two sonnets commemorating the death of Philip II.

1602   A sonnet for the *Dragontea* by Lope de Vega, and an ode to the Count of Saldana.

1605   The first part of *The Ingenious Gentleman, Don Quixote of La Mancha* was published in Madrid by Francisco de Robles.

1606–1608   Three sonnets: *To Don Alfonso González de Salazar, To a Braggart, To a Hermit.*

1610   A sonnet to the memory of Diego Hurtado de Mendoza.

1613   The *Exemplary Novels,* a sonnet for *First Part of Various Applications* of Diego Rosell, and some quatrains for Gabriel Pérez de Barrio.

1614   *Journey to Parnassus.*

1615   Stanzas in honor of Saint Teresa, and *Eight Comedies and Eight New Interludes.*

1616   The second part of the *Quixote* and the dedication to Count Lemos in *Persiles*, written on April 19, four days before his death.

1617   *The Trials of Persiles and Segismunda.*

INDEX